M000216439

The original *Théorèmes Poétiques* was first published in 1994 by Éditions du Rocher, © Basarab Nicolescu

© of this edition, Quantum Prose, 2016
Basarab Nicolescu's photograph by Louis Monier
Cover and inside photographs by Thomas Ahlgren

Editorial director
Marta del Pozo

Editorial advisors
Lissi Sánchez
Peter Kahn
Gregg Harper
Miriam Cruz
Luis González

Designed and edited by
Hugo Clemente

ISBN
978-0-9973014-0-3

Library of Congress Control Number
2016933359

Printed in the USA

Quantum Prose, Inc.
New York, NY

www.quantumprose.org

The Hidden Third

Basarab Nicolescu

Translated by
William Garvin

Foreword by
Gonçalo Tavares

QUANTUM PROSE

Table of contents

Foreword

Translator's note

Basarab Nicolescu, in this unusual and most excellent book, presents us with a kind of poetry that has its feet firmly on the ground, a ground which is at the same time scientific and philosophical. The poetic theorems in this *Hidden Third*, as the text itself suggests, are situated at "a point of convergence between quantum physics, Philosophy of Nature and inner experience." They explore the importance of a science that can see great distances - along with a more instinctive science of careful self-observation: "The forgetting of oneself by oneself gives rise to monsters" (XIII.50).

Life, the essence of all, provides the backdrop. It's the place from where we set out, as well as the destination where we hope to arrive. We think a great deal in order to live, and live long in our attempts to perfect our thinking. How rare, writes Nicolescu, are those who can master the essential: "I've known a great many doctors: doctors of words, of science, of lies, of dialectics, of nihilism, of philosophy. I've yet to meet a doctor of life" (I. 42).

These poetic theorems represent a synthesis, delivered in rapid phrasings, of human forebodings that are also a product of reflection. Foreboding arises before the appearance of something concrete.

Reflection arises later, sometimes much later, in relation to a specific event. Foreboding and reflection: two rhythms, two completely distinct methodologies, scare us but at the same time make us think. Which is why these perplexing theorems follow no specific order; straying from the imposition of any narrative sequence or fixed relationship between cause and effect that so often restricts digression. Here, by contrast, within these beautiful lines that Nicolescu has written - now happily published in English via Quantum Prose - we find ourselves in a field characterized by speed, a way of writing that shows only the effects and which doesn't submit to diminutive pre-justifications. Nicolescu advances and says what he has to say, fearless, without causes, and with no excuses.

Let's reflect upon the capacity for what these poetic theorems have to say. As I've said elsewhere, we should admire language as *a machine that initiates*, a linguistic machine that creates beginnings. A first phrase is always a first phrase: it begins. And in these poetic theorems, each theorem is always a first phrase. And the beginning, any beginning, always has additional force: it's always at the inception of a process where the greatest quantity of a substance is concentrated, something the development of that process is only going to dilute, or spread over a wide area.

Certain fragments, and Nicolescu's poetic theorems have the characteristics of fragments: force what is necessary to surface. They impose a sense of urgency, an impossibility of deferral. There's an *acceleration of language and thought*, with speed and mobility conjoining thought to necessity, which we see, for example, in poetry. Nicolescu writes: "Ambiguity rules the world. What greater ambiguity than that of "yes" and "no"? (X.2).

Thus in this book we find ourselves in a realm of sudden births and urgent necessities, returning to the visible in order to shatter and destroy. *The Hidden Third* seems to have been born out of an organic rhythm: a rhythm with no order, only necessity. It isn't by chance that the sixth theorem reads: "Freedom is discontinuity. Discontinuity gives meaning to the life of man" (I. 6).

This is, therefore, a book about freedom, a freedom both urgent and necessary.

Gonçalo Tavares
10/08/2015

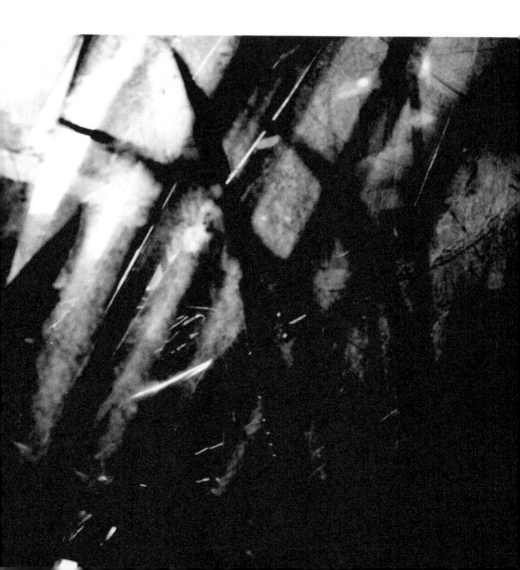

1

The Valley of Astonishment - the chasm between two levels of reality. The New Renaissance - the emergence of a reality encompassing several layers of reality.

2

The different levels of reality are energizing, which is why passing from one level to the next is necessarily discontinuous. Discontinuity is the condition for evolution. It's the exception that tells us about the norm, not the opposite.

3

Cosmic movement can be visualized as two parallel rivers moving with considerable force in opposing directions through all cosmoses. Discontinuity is precisely the crossing from one river to the next.

4

Without discontinuity there is no consciousness: without consciousness there's no discontinuity. Quantum discontinuity is one of the signs of cosmic consciousness.

5

The sudden appearance of being demonstrates the unpredictability of the unknown.

6

Freedom is discontinuity. Discontinuity gives meaning to the life of man.

7

Movement is born from a conflicting interaction between local and global causality. The nature of movement explains the existence of a ruthless law. Anything that doesn't evolve must necessarily degenerate and end up dying out.

An intelligible formulation regarding local causality: with each cause is associated, in the long term, an opposing effect to the one expected at the moment of action. Thus, the history of the world becomes understandable.

The living word: a bolt of lightning flashing in an instant across all levels of reality.

Each level of reality is associated with a very specific local causality. Thus miracles become possible, if not very probable. A miracle is the effect, conforming to laws, of one level of reality upon another. For example: the quantum miracle that makes the existence of the universe possible.

Practically all philosophers of all epochs have spent their time denying miracles. Naturally, we've succeeded in denying our own existence, which is the miracle of miracles. An elementary error of logic.

The word "tempest" evokes a (tumultuous and luminous) meeting between two levels of reality. Was it for this that Shakespeare wrote *The Tempest*?

The true meaning of celebration: the penetration of one level of reality by another. The world is filled with miracles. They constitute the poetic realm of existence.

The general principle of relativity is fundamental: the similarity in nature between man and nature is isomorphic to that between space and time.

15

Objectivity depends upon the level of reality. Objectivity associated with the macrophysical level is a pure and arbitrary subjectivity not acknowledged and not admissible.

16

The game of masks is not the mask of games. The game of masks is horizontal, it always takes place on a single level of reality, whereas the mask of games necessarily crosses several levels of reality, which is why the general principle of relativity is based upon the mask of games.

17

All tragedies in this world, from the tiniest to the greatest, have one and the same origin: non-acceptance of one's own place. The one exception: divine tragedy.

18

The word "universe" is inappropriate for describing our physical universe. There can't be several "ones" unfolding within a single whole. The idea of parallel universes - a charming fantasy and dangerous tranquilizer.

19

A single word - evolution - carries within it the entire universe. It's the word at the center of all the world's dictionaries. A word matrix for all other words.

20

Perpetual motion: evolution - involution. Evolution - the food of Absolute Evidence. Involution - the food of nothingness. A subtle asymmetry.

21

Good is anything serving evolution; evil, anything serving involution, which is why good and evil are inseparable.

22

Involution should be at the service of evolution, not the other way round. Otherwise Lucifer becomes Satan, bearer not of anti-sense but of non-sense.

23

Living time is the discontinuous time of evolution.

24

The void is our destiny. Born from the void, we occupy a void in order to head towards another void. The full void. From one hole to another - as the ancients used to say.

25

The quantum code is the code of the highway towards life. A little help. The highway towards consciousness remains unknown.

26

We don't descend from monkeys but from quantum particles. It's monkeys, therefore, that descend from man.

27

The sacred is anything tied to the evolution of consciousness. An ascending movement, energising and self-willed.

28

Consciousness implies a violation of the law of energy conservation. It isn't itself a miracle, but the manifestation of a miracle.

29

The mutilation of symbols is the pride and joy for archivists of the sacred.

30

Imposture doesn't have so much moral as cosmic significance. The inadequacy of energy-giving motion that creates order. Imposture brings about imposture. Posture brings about posture. Motion, therefore, always has two directions.

31

In order to escape imposture you have to change posture. It's a question of energy circulation.

32

Attitude is posture. The ability to maintain a certain bearing. Imposture is therefore the complete absence of attitude. Attitude always maintains the same sense: that of meaning, which is why it can change the world.

33

There are as many levels of perception as there are levels of reality.

34

Unity without man is a caricature. Unity through fusion is also a caricature. The unity of a single level of reality the worst of caricatures. However, there's no caricature without a model.

35

The anthropic principle is the bootstrap of the poor.

36

Freedom without constraint is not freedom.

37

The alienating complexity of one level of reality can be the harmonious simplicity of another. It's all a question of translation.

38

Man is the missing link between different levels of reality.

39

There's only one meaning I can attribute to the verticality of man: the perception of different levels of reality.

40
What does "I am" sound like at different levels of reality?

41
Man is the universe's observation instrument. In order to take his place, science has been given to him.

42
I've known a great many doctors: doctors of words, of science, of lies, of dialectics, of nihilism, of philosophy. I've yet to meet a doctor of life.

43
The multiple levels of reality can be arranged into two categories: hard reality and soft reality. Soft reality is concerned with reason and is explored by so-called "hard" sciences. Hard reality is concerned with man as an instrument of Absolute Reality and is explored by so-called "soft" sciences. A semantic reversal that's far from innocent.

44
Levels of reality, levels of knowledge, levels of consciousness - how does poor man find his bearings?

45
The basic contradiction of life: eating and being eaten. Food as the basis of metaphysics. The earth is a nourishing earth. Thus wars, large epidemics and death find their natural explanations. How do we find a way out?

46
Wise men of all ages tell us the evolution of man can only be the evolution of his consciousness. The superman is merely the hypothetical product of man's involution.

47
Outside - great particle accelerators; within - the great accelerator of consciousness. "Outside" and "within" are merely two facets of one and the same reality.

48
A taste for living - the simultaneous perception of all levels of reality.

1

Dictionaries tell us that "reason" is "the latin word that probably includes the most nuances and meanings." The wisdom of the ancients.

2

Why do they say that the sleep of reason engenders monsters? What reason are they talking about? The delirious logic of reasoning reason engenders just as many monsters.

3

The delirium of small reason is equal only to the delirium of great unreason. The mental - a receptacle of small reason. Necessary, though largely inadequate.

4

A sinister ruse of small reason: endless reasoning to take up an entire space. Small reason results from the contraction of reason to a single level of reality. An attempt to kill reason in the name of reason.

5

One more ruse of small reason: misinterpretation as meaning. The tyranny of small reason engenders tyrants, wars and self-destruction. The only way to fight the dictatorship of small reason is through reason itself.

6

The greatest discovery of modern man: the transplant of the mental from the human brain to electronic support. The mindset of the earth faced with the mindset of man - tragic confrontation or perverse complicity?

7

It is reasonable to pity reason's outcasts, but it's madness to forgive those who exclude different facets of reason.

8

Dialectical materialism isn't materialist. It postulates the existence of a single level of materiality. Dialectical materialism isn't dialectical: what circulates between opposites still remains opposed. So then, what is dialectical materialism?

9

Dialectical materialism is based upon the absolute dogma of binary logic, which is why everything said in its name became its opposite.

10

Working for power is the action of self-destruction.

11

The universality of binary thought is merely an illusion: the illusion of the Great Impersonator.

12

Frozen within fixed attitudes, hanging on to dead ideas, we're astonished life passes us by without waiting. Invited to a festival of knowledge, we content ourselves with a few scraps from the feast. Fragmented into a thousand realities, we advance from word to word, and then on again towards another word.

13

Contradiction - salvation or impasse? Binary contradiction is the impasse, ternary contradiction the salvation.

14

Mad irresistable laughter - an awareness of the contradiction inherent in any reality phenomenon.

15

The madman accepts contradictions without understanding them, whereas the wise man accepts contradictions whilst having an embodied vision of their unity. Thus, we can see why contradictory reason is often perceived as unsettling thought.

16

The Great Separator, The Great Impersonator, The Great Masturbator - three faces of the same god. A god created from our own mindset.

17

Dictators overrunning the earth - worshippers of The Great Masturbator.

18

We're told nature doesn't think. Perhaps. We're told science doesn't think. Perhaps. But then again, if only thought can think itself then it's obvious we can't be thinking our own thoughts.

19

The world's foundation is bottomless, which is why there can be no foundation to thought.

20

The tautological's despairing platitude wouldn't know how to live down its extraordinary efficacity: the mild tranquility of non-verticality is the cost. The tautological is the only science that gives a response to all questions great & small. It alone allows us to decipher the meaning of history. Is it a consequence of Einstein's space curve?

21

How do we comprehend knowledge, how do we know about comprehension?

22

Within the zone of contradiction a door to the infinitely conscious opens.

23

A problem as old as the world: how do you understand reason using reason? There is nevertheless a simple solution to this paradox: differing gradations of reason.

24

The only pathway towards understanding: the logical basis of the a-logical and the a-logical basis of logic. Any other discourse is mere chatter.

25

Everything to be understood is for the taking and everything not to be understood can do as it pleases. Thus, everything is understanding.

26

Not-knowing isn't so much ignorance as the surpassing of knowledge.

27

Before the chasm of the unknown there are two easy solutions:
1) replacing one enigma with another or 2) giving assertive responses, more or less embellished with logic. And, as ever, there's the Hidden Third.

28

Understanding is engendered through experience. Any explanation or theoretical generalisation is merely an approximation of this understanding.

29

The final theory is always and forever concealed within experience. Therefore it's forever inaccessible. Experience, however, is accessible.

30

The paradox of logic: its basis is empirical but its effect lies at the heart of being.

31

It is said that in theory you can say anything until proof of the contrary. But where is proof of the contrary?

32

The rational and the irrational are the two pillars of reason. Living reason includes the irrational. Otherwise you end up with a world of the living dead.

33

Irrational clarity compensates for rational obscurity. The complementary statement is also true, for there's only one source: the light of reason.

34

Light is what resides at the heart of mystery.

35

The engendering of one kind of logic through another or, more precisely, the engendering of various kinds of logic through nature, isn't that the most convincing sign of the irrational basis of rationality?

36

A child asks me: why was the word "infinity" invented? Seeing his look of despair, I can't respond with a mathematical lie.

37

To advance with joy and wisdom like a tightrope walker on a wire of the rational stretched across the middle of an infinite ocean of the irrational. For that matter, is there a middle to infinity?

38

Isn't wisdom quite simply the calm, rational acceptance, without any drama, fanaticism or nihilist hysteria, of the irrationality that's everywhere present, within ourselves and the world?

39

From the great word circus only one actor remains: the tightrope-walker.

40

The coherence of the irrational is equal only to the coherence of the rational. Reason has two aspects: great gnosticism and great science. Between the two - great poetry.

41

As its name suggests, metaphysics follows on from physics: theoretical metaphysics and experimental metaphysics are the two shutters of metaphysics.

42

The obscurity of impenetrable mysteries is total, but the pathway is nevertheless illuminated by their polarity.

43

What is worth more: the expression of an enigma, enigmatic expression or enigma pure and simple?

44

The secret of secrets: Absolute Evidence.

45

Wisdom is acknowledgement of the accomplished mystery.

46

The basis for a world without foundations is the absence of foundations. From where comes the responsibility towards self-genesis.

47

The first axiom of thought: what's fundamental will always remain fundamental, even with the absence of foundations.

48

The tiniest probability of the unexpected, as slight as it may be, is a sign of the presence of Absolute Evidence.

49

The word "evidence" (ex = on the outside, videre = seeing) is very ambiguous, for it depends upon space-time. What is the meaning of "seeing" in 137 dimensions? Absolute Evidence alone provides vision in non-space and non-time.

50

The best way to respond to an unanswerable question is to keep the question continually within yourself. That way it can feed on all possible responses.

51

The endless chain of unanswerable questions, from negation to negation and from affirmation to affirmation, leads to Absolute Evidence.

52

The Great Uncertainty Principle is the affirmation of Absolute Evidence.

53

Reason's games are endless: being, non-being as well as all degrees in-between (being and non-being), (neither being nor non-being), nor (neither being or non-being). What does it matter? Living. Endlessness.

54

Absolute Evidence isn't evidence of the absolute, but rather the absolute of evidence.

55

A difficult choice: the heaven of a question or the tomb of a response?

56

The logic of all logics is Absolute Evidence. It therefore can't be formulated. The logical basis for Absolute Evidence is extremely simple: neither (one or the other), neither (one nor the other), neither (one and the other), neither one nor the multiple.

Belief based upon faith can engender monsters. Faith based upon belief certainly engenders monsters. Only faith without belief gives access to Absolute Evidence.

Direct perception of reality should not be encumbered by the presence of intermediaries.

Beliefs are crutches helping us climb from one level of knowledge towards another.

The privilege of great prophets - proclaiming Absolute Evidence. The joy of false prophets - mistaking fantasy for Absolute Evidence.

How to make way for Absolute Evidence? We're too encumbered by nothingness. The passion of doubt, correctly channelled, can lead to Absolute Evidence. Otherwise we end up with nothingness, which is why nothingness and Absolute Evidence are so easily confused.

Sight distinguishes objects, vision illuminates sight, reality illuminates vision. From light to light we arrive at Absolute Evidence, the light-matrix of all light.

Communion and communicate both have the same root:
communicare = to be in contact with. Dictionaries don't tell us who or what we should be in contact with. To receive communion: seeing without seeing, looking without looking, understanding without trying to understand. Quite simply, acknowledging laws.

64

Contact with Absolute Evidence engenders infinite lucidity within infinite intoxication.

65

The meaning of baptism: immersion in Absolute Evidence.

66

Absolute Evidence has a quantum nature. It's not revealed reality: it's through a quantum leap we fall into its arms.

67

How do we choose between the knowable and the unknowable? The unknown gives life to knowledge.

68

The talent of great communicators: seeming to talk about the known starting from the known. In truth, it's the unknown they make arise, starting from the unknown.

69

Why is the naming of things the crucial act of comprehension or incomprehension? Because it's the power that acts through words.

70

There are three kinds of food for thought: accidents, relics and invariants. It's their impossible digestion or perfect assimilation that engenders great revolutions.

71

(Intelligence, negligence, religion) - (inter-legere, nec-legere, re-legere): one and the same root. The sublime wisdom at the origin of certain words.

72

A dictionary word: intelligence means literally "to read between the lines" ("inter-legere"). Should God's spies be tried for collusion ("intelligence") with the enemy?

73

Intelligence is acknowledgement of the unexpected.

74

Belief is the intelligence of the poor. As is unbelief.

75

Intelligence is not elitist: it is open to all, for it opens us all. Why not teach Socratic dialogue in our universities?

76

Nothingness is engendered by negligence. Its existence can only be phantasmagorical.

77

Religion: re (again) - legere (to gather). In its origins the word meant "scrupulous attention." Religion, therefore, could mean action endlessly renewed to receive attention. There's no authentic religion without the presence of attention.

78

Beliefs pass, religions remain. The understanding of nature will replace all belief.

79

One day it may be necessary to rewrite the great religious texts of humanity, replacing each word with its opposite. Thus, with the help of the Hidden Third, we'll perhaps manage to understand their meaning.

80

What's the difference between pagans and believers? The chasm of a few texts.

81

On the importance of dogma: mummification invariably conceals a corpse.

82

To understand reality is to understand at the same time the receptacle of this reality, which is why hell is so often present. Everything goes in circles.

83

A troubling enigma: is it man who observes the universe or the universe that observes man?

84

Binary logic is reversible: anything can be said as well as its opposite. Who is the arbitrator, wonders binary thought: nature or binary logic?

85

Everything in this world is related to everything else. Thus are engendered three dimensions of space. Our inescapable march towards physical death adds a dimension of time. The most tenacious dream of reason: the uniqueness of quadridimensional space-time.

86

How do we reconcile a-logical evidence of the indescribable with a logical approximation of the describable?

87

Spontaneity doesn't mean anything: there are degrees within spontaneity, as there are degrees within perception. Also, imagination doesn't mean anything. There are degrees of imagination, as there are degrees of reality. The contradictory polarity of imagination engenders the identity of the real. A complex conjugation, as in mathematics. Informed spontaneity and informed imagination create the basis for communication.

88

Sight cannot see reality. Only vision can lead us to its shores. The vision of reality - the reality of vision.

89

What is the light that helps us see? Physical light helps us to see objects and therefore survive. Inner light illuminates vision and makes us live.

90

Einstein's theory of relativity tells us there can't be any speed greater than that of the speed of light. What more evident proof of the limitations of our sight?

91

Intelligence is the capacity to read between the lines in the book of nature. Artificial intelligence is therefore an aberrant notion. It makes for an incredible preservation of intelligence. Two radical novelties: there's no use-by date and its volume can increase, in principle, to infinity.

92

The objects of quantum cosmology, paradoxically, are embryonic existences: germs, limbs, quarks, leptons, messengers. The universe as uncreated cosmos. It's therefore surprising when surprise is expressed at the metaphysical "drift" of certain scientists.

93

"Hypotheses non fingo " - what sublime vanity! Newton was a great seeker of Absolute Evidence. His only error: he was looking in a place where there wasn't any.

94

The first revelation of big-bang: an explosion in equations.

95

A bridge between the unknown and the unthinkable: the Hidden Third.

Thus the known and the thinkable are born.

96

The impenetrability of God is a sign that we are penetrable.

97

The Eucharist is Absolute Evidence's action of grace.

98

It is vain to seek proof of transcendence. How can you prove what is through what isn't? Absolute Evidence is not transcendence but merely the image of transcendence in the mirror of our being.

99

The demonstration of God is a monstrosity, invented by lifeless thinkers.

100

There are so many metaphysical scandals, one wonders how the celestial hierarchy remains in place. Unless everything is merely a comfortable mask for our irresponsibility.

101

The buddhist principle of non-support from logic is very bizarre. Without leaning upon logic you can't arrive at the evidence for a-logic.

102

The western idea of unity in diversity and diversity through unity is isomorphic to the eastern idea of non-duality. Why set them in opposition to one another?

103

Vision is the opposite of sight, which is why Tiresias was blind.

104

Madness signals the threshold of a quantum leap of understanding.

The dazzling thought of an Antonin Artaud is perhaps the best illustration.

105

I believe that one and the same material source gives rise to madness and wisdom. The difference between madness and wisdom is merely a question of receptacle.

106

Is it wise to be wise in a world of madmen? Or is it wise to be mad in a world of madmen? The wise man is he who knows how to recognize and integrate his own madness as well as the madness of this world.

107

A dream that's always pursuing me. An oriental market, a bustle of people talking in whispers, the most diverse colors, an atmosphere of celebration and ceremony. It is said with insistence that a woman had an "illumination" - an extraordinary event. Before the crowd - three women. To right and left two women seated in lotus position. In the center the woman who had the experience of illumination suspended vertically in the air, her head towards the ground, her feet upwards. Is this, therefore, illumination?

108

Does illumination consist of a simple reversal of signs?

109

My true friends are lovers of Absolute Evidence.

110

The decline and disappearance of civilizations are connected to an imbalance between knowledge and being.

111

The transmission of unknowing is as important as the transmission of knowing.

112

My enemies accuse me of wanting to introduce a new scientism and a new rationalism. They are right. To the extent that the word "new" implies creative negation.

113

The great mysteries of this world are like great gravitational masses, even light bows down in their presence.

114

I'm often asked where I want to reach with my reflections. And, when I say "nowhere," liars believe it's a lie.

1

Modern science is the first rational adventure in search of the unknown. Far from being frightening, the unknown can be rewarding, providing encouragement for further adventures.

2

The first postulate of modern science: the existence of general, universal laws that are mathematical in nature. It presupposes man's knowledge of the entire universe.

3

The second postulate of modern science: the possibility of discovery, through experience, of universal laws that are mathematical in nature. By what miracle does the human mind comprehend the language of nature? Does man contain within himself the entire universe - past, present and future?

4

The third postulate of modern science: the perfect reproducibility of experimental results. As Charles Saunders Pierce observed, do we have to make an infinite number of experiments in order to be sure about the perfect reproducibility of experimental givens and the validity of a law?

5

What surprise is there when making such an evident observation that the rationality of modern science is based upon three utopian and a-logical postulates.

6

The genius of Galileo lay in respecting transcendence whilst reducing it to an operative aspect.

7

Was it coincidence that the Renaissance gave birth to modern science? Maybe the meaning of new birth resides there.

Science, meaning, evolution - everything said in just three words.

The importance of science in relation to other religious and philosophical approaches is that it's neither eastern nor western.

The incessant changing of scientific theories demonstrates the permanence of modern science's methodology. The only belief of modern science is in its own methodology, which is why it's open to tradition as well as all other domains of knowledge.

The grandeur of science resides within its own clear limits. The advantage of limits: they allow us to glimpse the limitless.

A great intellectual scandal: modern science, arriving at its own limits, tolerates and even demands an ontological opening.

The paradoxical character of contemporary science is to predict the unknown, starting indeed, from what is known but also starting from what is unknown. A tumultuous marriage between theory and experience. Thus, great surprises have engendered great scientific revolutions.

The resurrection of the idea of "cosmos" is the most remarkable event of the 20th century.

The relationship between the quantum particle and the universe gives rise to the self-genesis of our cosmos.

16

"...this confounded quantum leap!..." exclaimed Schrödinger during a meeting in Copenhagen in 1924. Nevertheless, Schrödinger was one of the founding fathers of the "confounded" quantum mechanics. Is "Confounded" a scientific concept? (confounded = "satané").

17

Is quantum non-separability a sign of universal non-separability? A gigantic step I can't make.

18

Fortunately, a good friend tells me, we don't live in the quantum world. Alas!...

19

Does a small fireball contain, potentially, a whole universe?

20

The full void of quantum physics faced with the void of nothingness in our heads - what rich fecundity! The hollow void of classical physics - an expression of our mental void. A necessary step, surpassed by contemporary physics.

21

Carefully distinguish between the unification, unity and uniqueness of the world. We are ready to look sympathetically upon attempts at unification, however, we have difficulty admitting the unity of the world. As for uniqueness, that scares us to the depths of our being.

22

The universe was previously an immense high energy laboratory. You could learn everything about the secrets of matter. But there were no physicists. The story of the universe is the best detective novel, epistemology and science fiction. The author, however, remains anonymous.

Cosmologists and quantum physicists should all be imprisoned for the crime of colluding with cosmic intelligence.

A very clear sign of the decline of science: the loss of momentum of theoretical particle physics as well as the impossibility (in the foreseeable future) of building great high energy accelerators. It would take a cosmic accelerator to restore life to particle physics! Or maybe a change of vision.

Knowledge emerges from the unity of the observer and the observed. Thought that limits itself to what is observed or the observer is not scientific thought.

Some have dared think the unthinkable: quantum physics as a source of renewal for philosophy. Even the founding fathers of quantum mechanics didn't dare take that step. Must nature remain the eternal servant to philosophy?

The grandeur of science - allowing evidence for the a-logical to emerge.

Ideology disguised as philosophy, religion or science - one more ruse of binary thought.

The determinist fantasy: the universe as puppet. The determinist God is a god without imagination. Mechanistic and reductionist determinism replace God through a physical universe. An interesting and fascinating caricature of God, as it leaves no place for freedom.

30

The supreme vanity of certain scientists - proclaiming the incapacity of science to access meaning. Vanity in the guise of humility. If they are right, we would have to replace the words "the scientific community" with the words "community of the defenders of non-sense."

31

"Science alone, reason alone!" - an advertising placard for pornographic modernity. The basis of scientism is nothingness, which is why the messianic promise of scientism is annihilation.

32

Scientism is necessarily pornographic: in proclaiming that scientific knowledge is the only knowledge possible, everything is reduced to fixed images of God's orgasm.

33

The modern mania of always seeking the caution of science is a perverse obsession, for the methodology of science imposes upon it insurmountable limits.

34

Two asymptotic poles of the postulates of modern science: reductionism and holism. The great battle between these two schools is laughable. Nature tells us they are both correct.

35

There are three kinds of sciences: those predicting the unknown from the known, those predicting the unknown from the unknown and finally those that preside over the unknown, starting at the same time from the known and the unknown. The unpredictability of the unknown could provide the basis for a new science. The unknown contains the known, whereas the known does not contain the unknown.

36

"Thêorema" means "spectacle." What kind of spectacle is shown to us by mathematical theorems?

37

Despite its exalted definition, mathematics is not filled with word-corpses or symbol-corpses. The isomorphism between the human brain and nature saves mathematics from disaster.

38

It is natural to consider mathematics as a human science for it represents the emergence of the brain of man. One can also understand why Galileo made a distinction between human mathematics and divine mathematics.

39

The logic of God is, by definition, a-logical, and the place where God resides is, by definition utopian, which might be the reason why the three postulates of modern science are a-logical and utopian.

40

The amorous meeting between mathematics and the Hidden Third gives rise to physics.

41

Science is digging its own grave in its refusal to admit the necessity of a new philosophy of nature. It's not science that will give rise to the new science but rather a new philosophy of nature, centered upon the interaction between man and nature.

42

A simple definition of soft sciences: those engendered by the human brain that is itself so soft. Hardness resides within nature, which is why the social sciences can very well be described as hard sciences.

43

Knowledge is the birth of both man and nature, which is why scientific knowledge does not mean the conquest of nature.

44

Modern science has eliminated man, while the new science will rediscover man. An anti - Copernican revolution, both saving and redeeming.

45

Certain founders of the anthropic principle talk of "anthropic selection." Still the same entropic fear of the anthropic.

46

The adventure of the unconscious leads to science. The adventure of the conscious also leads to science. The same science?

47

"Metaphysics": a word which means "with physics." Beyond physics but with physics. From where comes the metaphysical importance of physics as well as the material ("physique") importance of metaphysics.

48

The "dialogue" established today between science and religion makes one think of the Peace at Yalta. The two parties claim they have nothing in common and yet nevertheless they want to have a dialogue. A sharing of territories. A Yalta in the world of knowledge.

49

Tradition is the science of the singular, non-reproducible event. The source of tradition can be nothing other than metaphysics.

50

What is esotericism in the technoscientific era? Certainly not technoscientific esotericism, an impostor with a blooming facade. So what is it then?

51

The first postulate of tradition: the existence of universal cosmic laws of a symbolic character. It presupposes that the man who knows is at the same time known. Thus potentially man contains within himself all cosmoses.

52

The second postulate of tradition: the possibility of discovering through inner experience universal, cosmic laws of a symbolic character. Man understands the language of nature because, without man, nature can't live.

53

The third postulate of tradition: experimental occurences are always singular and non-reproducible. From where comes the necessity for transmission.

54

Some have difficulty understanding at the same time the thesis of the Christian origins of modern science, as well as that of its universality. Time and non-time are combined within the Hidden Third.

55

The enigma of science and tradition: knowing everything about nothingness whilst accepting it understands nothing about everything or understanding everything about everything whilst accepting it knows nothing about nothingness.

56

There's a one-to-one, contradictory correspondence between the three postulates of modern science and the three postulates of tradition, which is why modern science and tradition are isomorphic. The study of the universe and the study of man reinforce one another.

57

Consciousness without science can only be the ruin of man. A reciprocal theorem has already been formulated.

58

Science - love by proxy but love all the same. Tradition - knowledge by proxy but knowledge all the same.

1

The history of nature tells us about the birth of meaning.

2

I agree with Raymond Ledrut: there can't be meaning without a meeting between presence and absence. It's the contradictory relationship of presence - absence that gives rise to meaning. Without inner experience there can't be meaning. Inner experience reveals the presence of absence.

3

Meaning is the source of negentropy. Deprived of meaning we are, in effect, deprived of food: we head straight towards death.

4

We believe that meaning resides in our heads. Thus, preachers of tautologies have replaced priests. They've even invaded the world, which should therefore be filled with meaning. We need only look around to convince ourselves.

5

Attributing meaning to meaning is insane. For the insanity of meaning is contained within meaning itself.

6

It's not our heads that give meaning to the universe but rather the universe that gives meaning within our heads. Or rather, neither one nor the other. Or more precisely, one and the other.

7

It is wrong to maintain that language transformed the animal into man. Unless one believes that language creates meaning starting from nonsense and reciprocally.

8

Ourselves, the quantum particle and the universe - the dizzying journey of "noûs."

9

Great philosophers are great pleasure seekers. They make fundamental truths disappear one after the next. In order to spread the frightening global famine of meaning, and thus help us rediscover meaning beyond all meaning.

10

Poets are physicists of meaning. They use words as instruments to investigate what lies beyond words - universal nature, whose physical universe is merely one of its facets.

11

Meaning doesn't begin where words end, but wherever words are in harmony with man's other faculties.

12

The meeting between the poetic and the quantum gives birth to meaning.

13

Responsibility - responding to the call of absence, welcoming into oneself its loving presence.

14

Is it those who are as-yet-unconceived who can best tell us about the meaning of meaning?

15

The abolition of time gives rise to meaning, which is why we always seek traces of meaning within time.

16

Physical light sheds light upon the universe, whereas inner light sheds light upon the poetic universe, which is why the physical universe has no meaning. It's also why there can't be any meaning without the physical universe.

17

A child's reflection: if there's only ourselves giving meaning to life, then you have to conclude that the universe had no meaning before the appearance of man. The invention of sensible man therefore, would be senseless.

18

The meaning of man's life resides in his leaving traces. Like quantum particles in a bubble chamber. The invisible made visible.

19

Avoid at all costs the formidable trap of confusing the meaning of history with the history of meaning.

20

Contemporary debate about meaning makes me smile. Why can't the blind see the light? How can't the blind see the light? Without an answer to these two questions, there's no way out.

21

The paradox of words: sense organs never give access to meaning.

22

Epistemic under-development is the greatest international, even transnational threat, of death to our world.

23

The folly of man can at last be explained: man attributes meaning to everything that doesn't have meaning and attributes no meaning to anything that does have meaning. Here lies the root of wars, totalitarianism, fanaticism, violence, hatred, self-destruction - history, in short.

24

Contemporary problems with meaning that ignore modern science and tradition, are, in the best of cases, problems of non-sense, anti-sense or misinterpretation ("contresens").

25

The history of meaning is that of a triad: sense, anti-sense and non-sense.

26

In eliminating unanswerable questions, we spend our time passing from one tautology to the next. And then we're astonished not to find any meaning in our tautological existence.

27

Non-sense: tautology is the science of sciences. Stronger than any science, stronger than any religion, stronger than any philosophy. For it alone can demonstrate the existence of nothingness as the mirror of everything.

28

One of the jewels of binary thought: misunderstanding. You can get yourself killed through a misunderstanding. Any misunderstanding can be analyzed if projected onto three axes: sense, anti-sense and non-sense.

29

There's certainly a place for meaning: the included middle. But there's no time associated with meaning.

30

Selfish misunderstanding is the privilege of cunning stupidity. The role of cunning intelligence - to foil the cunning of misunderstanding. It's here where the secret of crowd manipulation resides.

31

Why do practically all seekers of meaning lead to nonsense? The world's absurdity only conveys the murder of absence.

32

The meaning of meaning is very precise: from involution to evolution. As for non-sense, it's the pride and joy for those with nothing to say. The last refuge of the harebrained: proclaiming the problem of meaning has no meaning. Which presupposes, of course, that they know what the word "meaning" means.

33

Evidence of good sense is not evidence of meaning, which is why any philosophy based upon good sense is a philosophy of anti-scientific and anti-humanistic non-sense. Despite the charm of appearances.

34

The most dogged illusion: the meaning attributed to words. The interaction of words is beyond words. Words, therefore, are meaningless. Unless one identifies tautology with meaning.

35

As a matter of fact, any spoken word is condemned, for it gives rise to a tangle of misunderstandings. Only words experienced through life give access to meaning. Even mathematics can't escape this poetic theorem.

36

His stomach reassures him. Plenitude and fecundity, which is why words should be torn open to engender living words.

37

Etymology can also become delirious, like anything connected with words: "cosmic" and "cosmetic" both derive from "Kosmos." Cosmic cosmetology and cosmetic cosmology - two disciplines of the future.

38

A word mystery: if "to forbid" ("interdire") is to speak inside ("inter-dire") or to speak between ("entredire"), what does its current meaning derive from? Is what's spoken between words so dangerous?

39

What is beyond words is beyond evil. But evil is everywhere present. To condemn words, therefore, would be senseless.

40

The only logical way of broaching the eternal problem of Good and Evil is to consider it as universal, cosmic and simple. A stick always has two ends, different though inseparable.

41

The divine deluge has been a very crude means to resolving the problem of Evil. Our modern deluges, potential but very much present, are far more sophisticated and aren't linked at all to problems of Good or Evil. The conclusions are obvious.

42

The most important human right is the right to meaning. The democratic character of meaning is obvious. No-one has an exclusive monopoly on meaning, which is why meaning provides a basis for future universal democracy.

43

A slight change of attitude, equivalent to a major revolution: considering oneself a participant in the movement of meaning and no longer its unique proprietor.

44

There can be no New Renaissance without a radical change of mentality. We need to start by setting free the imprisoned meanings of words.

45

One of the possible meanings of alchemy: transforming the binary structure of misunderstanding into the ternary structure of meaning.

46

Tombs are filled with responses to unanswerable questions. Nevertheless we stubbornly continue our search for meaning.

1

Transdisciplinarity is an attempt to rediscover an equilibrium between knowledge and being.

2

Transdisciplinarity is a radically new form of human thought engendered by scientific cosmodernity.

3

The general principle of relativity finds human expression in transdisciplinarity.

4

Transdisciplinarity, as a scientific approach, examines the interaction between exact sciences, social sciences and sciences of the Hidden Third.

5

The contemporary explosion of disciplinarities; inter, multi, trans and beyond clearly shows that we suffocate behind the closed doors of knowledge for the sake of knowledge.

6

At the end of specialization: incompetence. The different disciplines are not doorways to the unknown, but rather jealously guarded territories. The voyager of the unknown must commit himself to a narrow path belonging to none of these territories, in danger from guardians of all territories.

7

The transdisciplinary era will be one of generalists and tightrope walkers.

8

Neils Bohr was right: the principle of contradictory complementarity, formulated in particle physics, has a much greater general reach. The proof of this - transdisciplinarity.

9

Science, art and tradition are the living ternary of transdisciplinarity, which is why the seeds of transdisciplinarity have existed since the dawn of time. Awaiting the quantum leap.

10

The transdisciplinary era: first of all being, in order to receive and gather the living words of nature.

11

The only choice: self-destruction or planetary civilization. Only transdisciplinarity can give rise to planetary civilization.

12

The next paradigm will or won't be transdisciplinary. Transdisciplinarity: both affectivity and effectivity.

13

Transdisciplinary space is infinitely more extensive than intergalactic space.

14

Transdisciplinarity isn't aiming for an illusory unity of knowledge. The ternary interaction of knowledge is its only goal.

15

Transdisciplinarity gives rise to quantum transformations: religion into transreligion, history into transhistory, ethics into transethics. Thus, from quantum transformation to quantum transformation, peace will break out in this world.

16

"Pontifs" originally meant "builders of bridges." The transdisciplinary era will be one of pontifs.

17

The included middle and transdisciplinarity have always been closely associated. The future transdisciplinary society will necessarily be one of the included middle.

18

Transdisciplinarity is the root of a new tradition.

19

The transdisciplinary era will be an era of translators - those who translate what happens at another level of reality into our own macrophysical language.

20

The survival of humanity depends on the outcome of a fight between transdisciplinarity and anti-transdisciplinarity. The first issues at stake: education and transdisciplinary ecology.

21

To each phenomenon corresponds an anti-phenomenon, said Lupasco. It's therefore normal that the transdisciplinary mind gives rise to the anti-transdisciplinary mind. Anti-transdisciplinarity is the best objective ally of transdisciplinarity: its failure provokes the birth of transdisciplinarity. The meeting between matter and anti-matter gives rise to immense energy. It's natural to expect an infinitely greater energy from a meeting between transdisciplinarity and anti-transdisciplinarity.

22

Transdisciplinarity is based upon the logic of the included middle, whereas anti-transdisciplinarity is based upon Aristotelian logic.

23

Transdisciplinarity transforms nature into anti-nature.

24

Why the so noxious confusion between transversality and verticality? Transversality is nearly always horizontal.

25

What at the same time can be "through" and "beyond"? Trans.

26

Alfred Nobel was born too soon. In a civilized society there ought to be only two great prizes: one for transdisciplinarity and another for anti-transdisciplinarity. Not paid in money but with love.

27

Transdisciplinarity is threatened by premature death: becoming itself a discipline.

28

It's not enough to put "trans" everywhere in order to be transdisciplinary. An example: "transcendence" is not a transdisciplinary notion, but the approach to transcendence can be transdisciplinary.

29

In the modern university they teach everything except universality. Why, in this world, does everything become its opposite? The university is by definition, a place for the study of universality, which is why the transdisciplinary university represents a return to source.

30

The basis of ethics can only be transdisciplinary.

31

The only universal language is translinguistic communication.

32

We're all transnationals before the eternal. Transnationals have no need for earth: the earth is their earth. But their territories are occupied by stupidity.

33

In former times the Internationale aroused so many hopes. Will the Transnationale be sung one day in the streets of all the countries of the world?

34

The only realistic approach these days is utopian.

35

The transpoliticians of tomorrow should start their education at transdisciplinary nursery school.

36

In transpolitics there'll be neither right, nor left, nor center. Its geometry will be isomorphic to that of the universe: the center is everywhere and nowhere. Transpolitics isn't geometrical but topological: it can't depend upon the system of reference. Local history is not an invariant of nature.

37

Political thought can take its inspiration from nature. In contemporary physics the notion of object is replaced by the event, the relation, the interconnection. Thus the scene is set for transpolitics.

38

Geometrical concepts fluctuate. The left isn't necessarily to the left, the right isn't necessarily to the right and the center isn't necessarily centered, which is why topological transpolitics should replace geometrical politics.

All those who know are to the right: all those who don't know are to the left, which is why the future belongs to the Hidden Third.

The only effective political will is poetic will.

Transhistory is the history of all histories. There's a book of history, just as there's a book of nature. Transhistory - movement between the lines of the book of history. A reading of the invisible rendered visible. Transhistory tells the history of the Hidden Third.

Differences between East and West are from another age. In the transdisciplinary era there'll only be nascent dawn.

It may be necessary to put history into the madhouse. But would humanity be able to invent a history beyond history? Transhistory is not the abolition of history. That's one more error from the metaphysical nihilists. An error of logic and, even worse, an error of style.

Transfigurative art is the art of the transdisciplinary era.

Objective art is art that awakens the dead.

Transreligion is neither the unification of religions, nor a unique religion or even less a religion of the unique. Transreligion is quite simply a religion of intelligence.

47

Nature is by definition, transnational and transreligious.

48

Transhumanism means: everything at the service of man, even God. Transreligion means: everything at the service of God, even man. Their relationship remains somewhat obscure. Unless it's merely a question of equivalence.

49

The door of the unknown opens towards transhumanity, a living nucleus of life on earth.

50

Transreligion is the logic of transcendence: theological truth.

51

The foundation of the rights of man: freedom, love, transdisciplinarity.

52

In the transdisciplinary era, the world will be filled with the silence of the poetic word.

1

Poetic knowledge is quantum knowledge of the Hidden Third.

2

There's a very simple definition of poetic space-time: space-time engendered by the interaction between all cosmoses. It's therefore unobservable and perceptible at the same time, both intellectual scandal and inner necessity.

3

Is the quantum imagination a unique example of the poetic imagination or the poetic imagination a unique example of the quantum imagination? There is, as always, a third possibility: the poetic imagination is none other than the quantum imagination.

4

Imagination is a fold within the real and the real a fold within imagination. From fold to fold poetic man has been invented.

5

Quantum imagination is the energizing circulation between two or more levels of reality linked by discontinuity. Poetic inspiration is the perception of interdependent breathing between different levels of reality.

6

From all evidence, words are quanta, shedding bountiful light upon contradictions between spoken and unspoken, sound and silence, actual and potential, heterogeneous and homogeneous, rational and irrational. The contradictory complementarity integrated within us by the Hidden Third.

7

The femininity of the poetic surrenders all of its meaning to the virility of the quantum. What the poetic and the quantum have in common: imagination. The difference between the poetic and the quantum: reality, which is why their meeting is so fruitful.

8

A wondrous quantum/poetic effect: if you request a precise temporal location for a quantum event, the result is that the expansion in energy must be infinite. Poets and philosophers have always felt that the idea of the immediate present contains within it an idea of primacy.

9

The rigorous poetic approximation of a scientific concept is very special. It confers, in its approximation, richness and infinite depth.

10

Capturing the ineffable: a contradiction in terms. The scientific act and the poetic act proceed, therefore, from one and the same process.

11

Poetry is the highest quantum approach in the world. Quantum mechanics depicts the mechanics of the universe, whereas poetry reveals its dynamic secret.

12

The quantum imagination: imagination without images. Or rather: imagination whose images surpass anything sense organs can conceive. Where is the source of images not engendered by sense organs?

13

Poetic matter is the energy of cosmic unity. Thus, even the most humble poetry has a cosmic dimension. Like a grain of sand containing an entire universe.

14

In addition to the four physical interactions you would have to add a multitude of others, including poetic interaction. Only then could you start to dream of a unified vision of the world.

15

Poets are quantum researchers of the Hidden Third. The rigor of the poetic mind is infinitely greater than that of the mathematical mind. It would be more appropriate to call research of the Hidden Third "exact science" and mathematics "social science."

16

Poetry - the opening up of language towards the Great Game. The dice game of the Great Indeterminate.

17

Poetic space-time is a trace within space and time of non-space and non-time.

18

A magical equation: Science + Love = Poetry.

19

A necessary alchemy: the metamorphosis of concept into poetic fact.

20

Crime against poetry brings with it all other crimes. Yet we don't punish it, for then the world would become a vast life prison.

21

On the fringes of non-being - great poets. Dropouts from being, tramps of the indescribable, beggars of love - those who take the blame - the Malamati.

22

Great creation is like possession: something speaks through us. New exorcists won't hesitate to appear.

23

Why do believers always talk of creation but never about poetic creation? Are they ashamed of the poet God?

24

If the big bang is scientific fantasy, then we're certainly poetic fantasy. How do we reconcile the irreconcilable?

25

Everything in life is a balance of power. Except poetry, which concerns the force of proportions.

26

Which is the more interesting language: one in which nothing vague can be said in a precise manner, or one in which nothing precise can be said in a precise manner?

27

The insurmountable difficulty of conversation: navigating different levels of knowledge.

28

The source of the prostitution of words: an infernal linkage from abstraction to abstraction. Making love purely with the mental. Bodies forgotten, feelings forgotten. Dead words.

29

Virgin thought is thought without words.

30

The death sentence of a word: its definitive definition.

31

Don't confuse rigor with exact definition. Too many definitions kill rigor, which is why poetic knowledge is more rigorous than scientific knowledge.

32

Words aren't made to be spoken, but rather to be thought, felt, looked at. In other words, a spoken word is an accursed word.

33

Words start to take on meaning, and therefore life, when they connect with scientific experience and inner experience. Generally speaking, this meaning is not found in dictionaries.

34

The shortcoming of dictionaries - the definition of a word demands the definition of all other words and carries, in fact, gigantic energy: the interaction of all words. The bootstrap of words.

35

The expression "etymological origin of words" is deceptive. There's only one origin of words - the lost word. Words are merely visible traces of the lost word.

36

Word gems - the joy of communion.

37

Living words are a necessary condition though not in themselves sufficient for a universal language.

38

There can't be a dictionary of living words. Unless we consider nature a cosmic dictionary.

39

Poetic theorems - a point of convergence between quantum physics, the philosophy of nature and inner experience.

40

Poetic theorems prove nothing: they exist to be experienced. The role of poetic theorems is not so much to open up as to allow penetration, which is why poetic theorems are not aphorisms. Poetic theorems don't demonstrate anything: they unveil the Absolute Evidence hidden everywhere.

41

Poetic theorems are not to be understood - they allow us to do as we please. Unless doing as we please is itself a form of understanding.

42

Poetic theorems do away with the vulgarity of word games. They seek the words of the game of nature.

43

Poetic theorems provide the only possible language for a non-vulgar popularization ("vulgarisation") of science.

44

Poetic theorems - the only means of extending Gödel's theorem to all other domains of knowledge.

45

Is there one modern poem comparable to Gödel's theorem?

46

Poetic theorems are the only means of spreading the great principles of physics to other domains of knowledge. To the great misfortune of the international community of scientists.

47

Life as a work of art: a day without poetic theorems is a definitively wasted day.

48

How could the first men on earth survive without poetic theorems?

49

Glossolalia is the first step towards a language of poetic theorems.

50

A good definition of poetic theorems was given (unintentionally) by Minkovski, when he spoke of Dirichlet: a minimum of blind formulas connected to a maximum of visionary ideas.

51

The asymmetry of reversible poetic theorems shouldn't surprise us: it's through breaking the symmetry of interaction between words that meaning arises.

52

My first love, my great love, my unforgettable love: Omar Khayyâm.

53

The Malamati - those who take the blame - were pelted with mud, persecuted, imprisoned and murdered for the crime of enouncing poetic theorems. Shams of Tabriz - our great companion before the Eternal.

54

The Zeami triade "jo" (opening) - "ha" (break) - "kyu" (paroxysm) is one of the most beautiful poetic theorems ever stated: johakyû.*

---

* "johakyû"is a law introduced by Zeami (1363–1444), one of the first great masters of the Noh theater. 'Jo' means 'beginning' or 'opening,' 'ha' means 'middle' or 'development' (as well as 'to break,' 'crumble,' 'spread out'), and 'kyu' means 'end' or 'finale' (as well as 'speed,' 'climax,' 'paroxysm'). According to Zeami it is not only theatrical performance itself which can be traced down into jo, ha and kyu, but also every vocal or instrumental phrase, every movement, every step, every word (BN).

55

Why are there so few poetic theorems within the extraordinary magma of written and spoken words since the dawn of time? Is Absolute Evidence so scarcely evident?

56

Commentaries about poetic theorems are not poetic theorems, whereas poetic theorems about poetic theorems are always poetic theorems.

57

Poetic theorems, prophetic theorems or axioms of Absolute Evidence? Must we choose?

58

Absolute proof for the existence of God: it's not God but poetry that created the world.

59

The only subversion that can make this world explode: poetic subversion.

60

The difference between terrestrial man and cosmic man is as great as that between the monkey and man, which is why all countries should create a Ministry for Cosmic Affairs, administered by poets.

61

Stronger than cyclones, tornados, floods, epidemics or innumerable bombs, poetic insurrection will sweep through this world like the blinding light of love. In the name of the rights of cosmic man.

62

My only riches are poetic theorems. And I give them to the rich.

1

Modern physics is no longer the physics of modernity. Cosmodernity is the return of modernity to its source.

2

Is there a worse barbarity than that of non-contradiction?

3

Modernity is characterized by the binary separation of subject - object, whereas cosmodernity is based upon the ternary unification of subject-object-included middle.

4

The obscurity of negligence and the ambiguity of binary thought have transformed the world.

5

Slaves of binary thought we dream of loving everyone, of constructing and building a terrestrial paradise. And then we're surprised when we see hatred and self-destruction invading the earth, establishing hell everywhere.

6

Complete actualization is annihilation of the other, which is why binary logic lies at the root of the new barbarism.

7

Wars are always bipolar: East-West, North-South, right-left, Orient-Occident, high-low, rich countries-poor countries, one camp against another. What more dazzling proof of non-contradiction's barbarity than the impossibility of counting beyond "two"?

8

Why did the great talkers of the last century want to convince us, at any cost, that man is merely an accident within the history of the universe?

This way everything becomes permissible. Violence, war, self destruction of our species. Can accident have a destiny?

9

The binary degeneration of religions can only lead to their dying out.

10

When religion becomes negligent it denies its own nature. Thus we are present at the birth of ideology religions, fanaticism religions, anti-religious religions. What a godsend for mendicants of the sacred!

11

Our cheerful modern prophets of non-sense are merely binary logic's political commissars.

12

One of the unquestionable signs of modernity: the contempt for and even absence of femininity. What is the meaning of virility without femininity? The modern opposition between the virility of effectiveness and the femininity of affectivity leads to the abyss of self-destruction.

13

The wave of superlatives in contemporary scientific language - superunification, superspace, supergravity, superstrings, supersymmetry - a superb deception ("supercherie") on the part of binary logic?

14

Great ideological plagues have a logical basis. The only way to reveal their imposture, therefore, is to place oneself within another kind of logic.

15

The fiendish dialectics of binary thought have the redoubtable yet subtle force of being able to kill in the name of ideas. One example: dialectical materialism. Binary logic is based on the implicit hypothesis of absolute truth and absolute falsity. We can see why it lies at the source of all totalitarianism.

16

The founders of dialectical materialism advanced, masked beneath the false ternary thought of Hegel. Were they so ashamed of binary logic, or was there a fraudulent desire to blow up the immense energy of the Hidden Third? Both, maybe.

17

Objecting to great ideological plagues for aesthetic, moral or spiritual reasons is a necessary condition, though it doesn't suffice to bring about their downfall. Only the logic of the included middle can create their downfall.

18

History's dustbins and warehouses are filled with all the philosophical, ideological and religious systems that describe the path towards the happiness of humanity. What better demonstration that man alone cannot work for the happiness of humanity?

19

The last century has been absolutely deadly - the death of God, the death of the universe, the death of ideologies. Can death engender life?

20

Cosmic laughter doesn't necessarily mean optimism. Cosmic depression doesn't necessarily mean desperation. A major error by nihilists of all ages.

21

Can you be a nihilist and a metaphysician at the same time? All nihilists wear me out because they endlessly assert their own convictions. Nevertheless, there are some nihilists who do interest me, because their negation-affirmations bring an opening to light within one and the same question.

22

A non-poetic cosmos is an absurdity, for that would be its own negation. Yet we accept living on a non-poetic earth in the name of inexorable necessity. That of our own absurdity.

23

Closed to the joy of cosmodernity, fascinated by the dreariness of post-modernity - we advance slowly towards a black sun of despair.

24

Whoever introduced the word "computer" took inspiration from the expression "The Great Ordainer" ("Le Grand Ordinateur"). A deterioration of meaning so characteristic of our beloved modernity.

25

The subject-object separation allows for their perpetual inversion. A subject that becomes object: man. An object that becomes subject: the computer.

26

A disease of modernity: non-surprise. Words, charged as they may be, no longer surprise us. Wars, revolutions, countless diseases no longer surprise us. Even the disappearance of life on earth no longer surprises us, which is why non-surprise is a deadly disease.

27

The great fascination exerted by the irreversibility of time on modern thought is understandable, for it quite simply concerns a fascination for death disguised as immortality.

28

Prophets who have nothing to say in the name of science worry me far more than prophets who have nothing to say in the name of poetry or philosophy. Technoscience - what formidable power within the hands of black magic!

29

Miracles have nothing to do with power. The miracle is vertical, whereas power usually exerts itself on the horizontal plane. This is the major error of occultists who are more or less technoscientists and technoscientists who are more or less occultists.

30

The mental, a powerful means for the adaptation of man to his environment, became an end in itself. Our collective suicide is to be envisaged. The modern castration of affectivity can only give birth to nothingness.

31

The rule of quantity is the rule of binary thought.

32

Technoscience is a marriage against nature.

33

The drunken boat of technoscience sails in an unknown direction, in an unknown ocean, a carrier of all threats and all potential wonders.

34

Can technoscience have a soul?

35

The ultimate scientific dream: creating hell not within a laboratory, but on a worldwide scale. The experiment has already taken place.

36

A simple change of face or sex: for example, replacing God-the-Father with Goddess Reason. And then, in the name of reason, in the name of science, killing millions and millions of people.

37

Barbarous words overrun the world as necessity: technonature, technoculture, technoscience. Thus the way is now open towards technohumanity.

38

The schizophrenia of quantity - ritual murder.

39

For every alchemy there's also anti-alchemy. Modernity is the triumph of anti-alchemy: the transformation of gold into filth.

40

Without communion there can be no communication: the cannibalism of words and images replaces the Eucharist. The cannibal word and the cannibal image are the anti-divine couple of modernity.

41

In our age it's no longer the image that has to conform to reality, but reality that has to conform to the image.

42

Asexual metaphysics merely accentuates the noise of words.

43

There's something barbarous, rough and indecent in the sudden appearance of life. It's therefore difficult to understand why makers of great phrases are mistaken for great thinkers. Unless the genius of language be used merely to the advantage of vacuous thought.

44

The prostitution of words is the absolute weapon of modernity.

45

The world is filled with a noise barrage of words more formidable than weapons.

46

La pétomanie - the art of speaking without saying anything. This is how false prophets are born.

47

The noise of modernity has an anti-alchemical nature: it transforms metaphysics into pétophysics.

48

I don't understand those who say that words are inoffensive, that words don't bite. Yet words have already killed millions and millions of people.

49

Where is the seat of consciousness of the *pétomane*?

50

The excrement of words creates delight for prophets of nothingness.

51

Worshippers and deniers of God have one thing in common: they talk.

52

The stuttering of gods - the logorrhea of men.

53

Any word spoken to say nothing is an accursed word. The food of nothingness.

54

The prostitution of thought is the world's oldest profession.

55

Why do great ideas become their opposites in the mouths of the prophets of nothingness? Perhaps because they lack the flavour of Absolute Evidence.

Culture is the prehistory of intelligence.

From one kind of humanism to the next we've arrived at technohumanism, which is the negation of humanism: humanity in the service of technology. There's only one way out of the impasse: transhumanism.

Whilst severely criticising it, I'm not against modernity. I'm for cosmodernity.

The world is like a dustbin, ready to give whatever's left of its soul. Thus is engendered the immense hope for movement in an opposing direction.

There are several kinds of thought: journalistic thought, thought relating to trails and thought relating to remains. Journalistic thought is always on the lookout for fashion and news. Thought relating to trails seeks invariants of movement. As to thought relating to remains, it has the ambition of restoring God's orgasm, starting from his relics.

Modernity is based upon journalistic thought and thought relating to remains. Science and tradition are based upon thought relating to traces, which is why cosmodernity signifies the rediscovered unity of the ternary of thought.

A civilized world is a world which is at the same time quantum and poetic.

The disease of modernity: the non-existence of a new philosophy of nature in accordance with discoveries in contemporary science.

64

The passage from the universe-machine to a living universe is one of several signs of metamorphosis from modernity to cosmodernity.

65

Quantum discontinuity, indeterminacy, the randomly constructive, quantum non-separability, bootstrap, the unification of all physical interactions, supplementary dimensions of space, big bang, the anthropic principle - so many poems from this gigantic modern Mahabharata that plays out before our blinded eyes. I dream of a great director who would have the courage to cast Max Plank as the central character in the Mahabharata of cosmodernity.

66

The cosmic economy hasn't the same nature as the human economy. But one can take inspiration from the other.

67

An unexpected aspect of the nature of space-time: values that make the world evolve lie neither in the mediocrity of brilliance nor in the brilliance of mediocrity.

68

The error of all prophets ancient or modern: the future is neither before us, nor behind us.

69

Evidence for the reversibility of time: great texts of humanity, great works of art, great teachings. Time's arrow leaves no imprint upon them. But this testimony submits to no mathematical formalization.

70

There's only one permanent reality: the Hidden Third, which is why it's of no interest to journalistic thought.

Invent a quantum, transdisciplinary civilization or perish.

The error of modern philosophy: thought should be at the service of being and not being at the service of thought. Science, by its very nature, has avoided this error.

I hate the modern pleasure in word games, presented as great philosophy. But the words of the Great Game interest me to the highest extent.

The new ecology - a battle against the pollution of pétomanic prophets.

Refusing word games whilst accepting the youthfulness of words. Quantum poets against the great talkers. Cosmodernity - the worst insult against the great talkers of today.

The exploitation of man by man will disappear when the exploitation of words by other words is annihilated.

The only army in a future universal democracy will be one of poets: they will go and fight the holy war on all fronts.

The alchemists' Ouroboros anticipated the metamorphosis of modernity into cosmodernity.

The threat of the self-destruction of our species is salutary: it shows we're at the threshold of a new birth.

80

The space and time between any two points on earth are virtually abolished by the power of our data processing. To what cosmic necessity is the sudden appearance of a planetary brain a response? The power of data processing teaches us how, without even moving, we can go faster and faster - at the speed of light. Towards what destination?

81

Computers offer man a chance to abolish war, playing at war on a computer instead. Playful war.

82

The "religion-negligence-intelligence" triad - what an extraordinary tool for a comprehension of history (history of man, history of humanity, history of the Universe)!

83

Religious ideology is more dangerous than any other ideology, for it alone knows the great secret of the transformation of the living God into living fantasy. All ideologies of history have been the prefiguration of a great religious ideology, which is why the New Renaissance begins through the abolition of ideology.

84

Intellectual abstinence is worth more than intellectual masturbation. More important still, the abstinence of power is worth more than the masturbation of power.

85

Mathematical scientism, material scientism, philosophical scientism, religious scientism, scientism period - the same battle.

86

Without necessarily making appeals to etymology, it's evident that negligence is the negation of religion and intelligence is the negation of negligence. The absurdity of the world merely reflects our own negligence.

87

The deepest root of stupidity: negligence.

88

Cosmodernity - a sparkling demonstration of the modernity of tradition.

89

There's no community without tradition and no tradition without community.

90

The future universal democracy will have one fundamental law: unity in diversity and diversity through unity.

91

The end of history is only a fantasy engendered by negligence.

92

The majority of utopias were anchored in specific places - for example the whole world. They weren't therefore utopias. Ours is finally the time for utopia.

93

Waiting for Godot or the Hidden Third. The metamorphosis of waste into gold - the alchemy of cosmodernity.

94

A civilized society begins with the foundation of an academy for the secret agents of God.

1

Everything has a place in this world: Good and Evil, man and nature, God and the Devil, law and accident. Only stupidity has no place for it is, precisely, the confusion of places.

2

There's only one forbidden tree in the garden of Eden: the one of stupidity. By what miracle of dialectic have we reversed the words "stupidity" and "knowledge"?

3

Light is, at the same time, the beginning of knowledge and the beginning of ignorance. In between both sneaks foul stupidity, which is why stupidity is also a being of light.

4

The best illustration of the ontological catastrophe of stupidity - the fall of Lucifer, this vile beast of stupidity, disguised as a being of light. Why has the ontological catastrophe of stupidity escaped metaphysical theorists until now? Perhaps because unwittingly they associate "beast" and "stupidity" ("bête" et "bêtise"). Though correctly...

5

Everything has a use in this world, except stupidity.

6

Stupidity is born from evil, but it surpasses its master.

7

Stupidity is beyond good and evil: it tries to make us believe in the existence of a single level of reality. There's a big difference between stupidity and intelligence: stupidity is terrestrial whereas intelligence is universal.

The difference between man and beast: man is a creature of the universe, whereas the beast is a creature of man. A sign of the sovereign liberty of man, which is why the world can become a kingdom of stupidity.

The vile beast of stupidity's world resides within our heads. A small place, as big as the earth. Stupidity is engendered by total and irreversible identification. The paradox of stupidity: an incarnation of the negation of reason, it is nevertheless well concealed within the head of man.

Stupidity is absolute proof of the freedom of man.

The infinitesimal distance between stupidity and wisdom: at the origin of stupidity lie two words - I and me; at the origin of wisdom, only one - I.

So-called sincerity is a manifestation of stupidity: blindness to oneself, closure of one's relationship to the other, disregard of cosmic laws. Idolatry of mechanicity. Sincere automatons killing one another in the name of stupidity.

The confusion between evil and stupidity is pernicious: evil is only one of the many faces of stupidity.

Confusion of languages is just one example of the confusion of places.

We still have a chance: stupidity is not a hereditary disease. There is nevertheless a strong heritage of stupidity. It will vanish one day like a shameful disease that's finally been eradicated.

16

It's unhealthy to confuse madness with stupidity. Madness is the highest state of ordinary man, whereas stupidity is his lowest state.

17

Madness has the great advantage of making us blind to the world's stupidity. But, at the same time, you only see your own world. At the opposite pole, wisdom watches both the world and the world's stupidity with a disinterested eye.

18

The most cunning figures in history - Hitler, Stalin and their kind - were not madmen, but rather the incarnation of absolute human stupidity.

19

A brief classification for all garbage cleaners: innocent garbage, conscious garbage, victim garbage, crackpot garbage, sinister garbage, recoverable garbage, irrecoverable garbage, brilliant garbage, obscure garbage, dogmatic garbage, transgarbage. To be displayed in all churches.

20

The supreme ruse: building a theory upon a non-defined theory. The lie has, as its basis, a non-defined double negation. Its incarnation is so-called new man.

21

Stupidity's best weapon is the cunning lie. Based upon truth, it extends its filaments deep into the sleep of reason's darkness. Thus the cunning lie is stronger than any truth.

22

There's an obvious relationship between lies and stupidity: an implicit or explicit negation of the levels of reality. In fact, the lie is stupidity's logic for taking possession of the earth.

23

The essential characteristic of chaotic logic is that there's no other value of truth than the lie itself. Even Great Liars don't know the truth of which they are guardians. Chaotic logic has only one aim: taking power.

24

Today Great Liars have replaced Great Priests. Still for the happiness of men.

25

Those we call "intelligent people" are often merely brilliant apostles for the obscurity of stupidity.

26

The confusion of places has no place in the search for verticality.

27

Words always deceive. The logic of the included middle is one of exclusion - an exclusion of stupidity. The conclusion is apparent: the logic of the Hidden Third is one of inclusion.

28

The only hatred that seems justified to me is that of the absolute singular and that of the absolute plural. In other words - hatred of stupidity.

29

The peak of impotence is the peak of stupidity. A good example: the so-called conquest of nature. It means the annihilation of our own nature.

30

The most indubitable sign of stupidity: confusing the Eucharist with cannibalism.

31

The youth of humanity in comparison with the great age of the universe is an excuse for stupidity. You would have to deduce from that that we need to reach the same age of the universe in order for humanity to become, like the universe, a humanity-relic.

32

The only way to safeguard stupidity is to kill the world's poetry. The only means of living the world's poetry is to recognize the true nature of stupidity.

33

The great terrestrial prison created and guarded by stupidity has very thick walls. All escape is impossible. The only means of release: convincing the guard himself to leave, with sweetness, with love, with tenderness.

1

Stubbornly seek the foundations for a world without foundations.

2

Nature - "natura" - "state of birth" - birth of God - birth of intelligence. Some are surprised we can talk of living nature. They're right, for it's a pleonasm: the word "birth" ("naissance") is found within the word "nature."

3

Nature is a pre-text. The book of nature, therefore, exists not to be read but rather to be written.

4

How can we be blind to the double nature of nature, be it naturing or natured?

5

The double nature of naturing nature, the double nature of natured nature and their interaction gives rise to a true ternary: supernature, intermediary nature and creaturely nature.

6

The triple nature of nature engenders different levels of reality; different levels of reality engender different degrees of reason; all degrees of reason are unified within nature's imagination.

7

There's a favorable direction for our cosmos: one leading towards a densification of energy, towards unity in diversity, towards an increase in consciousness. It's that which introduces the symmetry nature - anti-nature.

8

The triple nature of nature corresponds with the triple nature of anti-nature. Thus is born the first nonary, which explains why ascension is always so difficult.

9

There are three cosmic nonaries: the first engendered by the interaction of nature and anti-nature, the second through the self-interaction of nature, and a third through the self-interaction of anti-nature. These three nonaries engender all cosmic complexity.

10

Sight belongs to the world of creaturely nature, vision to the world of intermediary nature and reality to the world of supernature. Absolute Evidence sheds light upon all at the same time.

11

The Hidden Third acts within intermediary nature. It creates a bridge between creaturely nature and supernature.

12

The place of the imaginal is supernature.

13

Nature is an invention of supernature for its own protection. Any path towards supernature therefore, is necessarily counter-nature.

14

One of the worst confusions: the one between counter-nature and anti-nature.

15

The first letter in nature's alphabet: evolution. The final letter: Absolute Evidence.

16

The human adventure - reading the alphabet of nature starting at the end and ending at the beginning: from Absolute Evidence towards evolution. The progression of man is therefore counter-nature.

17

The involutive entropy of humanity is the price to pay for creaturely na-
ture's evolutionary negentropy. It's in this, and only this sense, that we can
affirm that the individual evolution of man is a counter-nature process.

18

The three aspects of nature coexist within any reality phenomenon,
but the predominance of one aspect or another gives rise to different
cosmoses.

19

Lupasco said that affectivity is the transcendence of energy. Does
affectivity imply trans-nature?

20

Nature, anti-nature, trans-nature - can a living God escape the effect of
this triad?

21

Maybe our world can be symbolized by a triangle, whose base represents
our gaze at the world and ourselves, the two other sides our inner lives
and our relationship with nature. Maybe this triangle can be reduced to
a single point: nature.

22

The ungroundness is the basis for any manifestation, for any process, for
any event. How do we plunge into the ungroundness without losing our
minds? By taking nature as our companion and guide.

23

O.W. de L. Milosz tells us "the smell of silence is so old.... " What more
precise formulation of our kinship with the ungroundness?

24

The Creator is the first creature of the ungroundness, which is why creators return to the ungroundness.

25

The universe being engendered by the ungroundness, one could conclude that the big bang was an immense silent explosion of the Great Silence.

26

We can't conceive of a richer automorphism than that of the ungroundness. Universal interdependence is merely an echo of this automorphism.

27

True movement is one of energy.

28

Contradiction is omnipresent energy's necessary transformation from one quality to another. A world without contradiction is doomed to die.

29

The history of the universe tells us that non-differentiated energy is the substrate of any manifestation.

30

The uselessness of the notion of object: the object is merely a local configuration of energy.

31

The only information worthy of the name: energy-giving information. It's that which gives form to the as-yet-unformed.

32

Energy is a unifying concept: information is a coded form of energy, whereas substance is its visible condensation, which is why any distinction between material and immaterial only rests upon terminological confusion.

33

Lucidity: becoming aware of the formidable energising struggle taking place all the time within nature.

34

Love has an energy-giving resonance, which is why there are as many kinds of love as there are kinds of energy.

35

A cosmic law: the densification of energy is always associated with an increase in consciousness. The existence of atomic bombs shows that man is capable of violating this law.

36

Human history can be defined as a progressive diminution of consciousness, in favour of an increase in power of man over nature. This entropic involution is the basis of self-destruction.

37

Non-differentiated energy from the "beginning" of the big bang is certainly an energy of unification, even if it's not perhaps the energy of unity.

38

The energy of the Great Silence is inexhaustible, which is why the energy crisis is merely a noxious human fantasy. For example, the fantastic energy at the moment of the big bang shows that the universe has never experienced any energy crisis.

39

God's orgasm isn't the appeasement but rather the maximal intensification of an energizing antagonism.

40

Why is there so little matter in the universe? Perhaps because the living matter found on earth would suffice the universe several lifetimes.

41

Matter - anti-matter - transmatter: three facets of one and the same matter. Affectivity is absolute transmatter, intangible and inconceivable. From this point of view, everything that exists in the universe is material.

42

Transmatter is not subject to involution: it can only evolve.

43

The dazzling perversity of the stars: concealing evidence of the invisible.

44

There are three lights: the light of supernature, the light of intermediary nature and the light of creaturely nature.

45

Light falls on earth as on all other bodies. Its fall shows us its nature: the anti-light of a light so much sought after.

46

Always the same question: discovering what lies between darkness and light. Why, since the dawn of time does the enigma remain unsolved?

47

Light is very old, for it's been in our universe since the dawn of time ("la nuit des temps"). But how precisely, on such a dark night with no photons, could the universe see itself?

48

One can easily imagine a photon without man, but it's impossible to conceive man without the photon. The disturbing asymmetry of light.

49

Light is the true messenger of the universe. But it's not aware of the message it carries, which is why any idolatry of light is an act of ignorance.

50

An adolescent looks at his image in a mirror and a question arises in him: what would his image look like if both he and the mirror could travel at the speed of light? Suddenly he realises he'd no longer see anything. The name of this adolescent was Einstein.

51

If light could dream, what would be its greatest dream? Seeing.

52

The absolute transparency of transcendence renders sight impossible but it does permit the birth of vision.

53

Man and nature have something in common: a gaping hole towards the unknown, from where comes a fascination for laws. Laws of the unknown.

54

Freedom lies within rigor, rigor lies within freedom.

55

Don't confuse nullity with zero. Nullity is downfall, whereas zero is noble elevation. The origin of one is human whereas the other is cosmic. Yet both are expressed by the same majestic number: 0.

56

The universe appeared through an infinitesimal change from zero. This is how matter was created. Anti-matter was cast into a hell of light.

57

What's up above is like what's down below, but unfortunately what's below doesn't resemble what's up above. A hermetically closed asymmetry.

58

Freedom is violation according to laws, arising from these same laws.

59

Laws are the result of divine collaboration: God invents symmetries and the Devil their breakages. This is how the world goes: from nothingness towards matter. Only man can reverse the flow.

60

Great symmetries are as universal as their breakages. An infinitesimal breakage can engender a world.

61

A respect for laws imposes their discreet violation. This is how being was engendered, starting from non-being - the cosmos starting from the quantum void - and life starting from non-life.

62

The disclosure of cosmic secrets is only possible through a breakage of symmetry, as infinitesimal as it may be: matter - anti-matter, unity-diversity, man-woman. Original sin is therefore a sin of asymmetry.

63

The role of the biblical serpent is one of blinding simplicity: causing an outbreak of cosmic asymmetries, which is why we come across him again as Ouroboros - a symbol of fulfilment of the great alchemical work.

64

Laws of nature are made to be broken. Very discretely, out of a respect for laws. An interesting lesson about freedom.

65

The first principle of the world's dynamics is extremely simple: everything that can happen happens, which is why there'll never be a theory that can espouse all the richness of nature.

66

The most magnificent and alarming aspect of this world is the principle of maximality: if we wait long enough, everything happens. Even miracles, even the worst horrors.

67

The principle of maximality is a means invented by God to ensure the reciprocal feeding of all levels of reality.

68

Three magic words in order of obscurity: unification - all interactions tending towards one and the same interaction; unity - each level of reality is what it is because all other levels of reality exist at the same time; uniqueness - equations of cosmic processes have a unique solution. Of course, it doesn't mean that our world is the best of all possible worlds.

69

Certainly, nature's dice are loaded: it's always the One that turns up, parent and child at the same time.

70

The arithmetical 1 has a special characteristic: any number, even an infinite number, multiplied by 1 always gives the same number. Similarly, any process associated with the metaphysical One still remains the same, though it is secretly enriched by the cosmic whole.

71

The miracle of unity is as great as that of diversity.

72

The bootstrap of quantum particles is merely one facet of a self-consistent intelligence linking galaxies, the quantum world, stars, man, planets, atoms and all cosmoses.

73

Cosmic democracy: an event is what it is because all other events exist at the same time.

The unification of physical interactions (moreover hypothetical) is merely a far off echo of the Great Cosmic Unification. The so-called theory of "everything" in physics is only an approximation of the Great Cosmic Unification. The fact that it meets considerable difficulties only reinforces its status as a necessary and useful approximation.

Universal interdependence is inscribed within nature.

There are two kinds of law: laws concerning the system as a whole and laws concerning constituent parts of a system. It necessarily follows that a third kind of law must be present.

Non-separability is the safeguard of life.

The innate is anything relating to the whole universe, whereas the acquired is anything relating to local environment, which explains why man is the most extraordinarily unsound creature between heaven and earth.

The trialectical wisdom of words: "kosmos" means "the order of the universe, of worlds." Worlds from worlds give rise to cosmoses. The ensemble of cosmoses forms the universe.

Complexity is a measure of the distance between man and God.

The anthropic principle proclaims, in a roundabout way, the action of supernature within creaturely nature, which is why, despite its scientific basis, its conclusions are not scientific.

82

In the absence of the infinitely conscious, the word "complexity" irresistibly evokes the image of an immense rubbish tip. When it's said that man and the universe represent the crowning glory of complexity, we must conclude that the modern cosmological narrative is telling us the story of a cosmic rubbish tip.

83

It may be necessary to talk of "ordered complexity." One quantum particle is infinitely more complex than an interplanetary rocket. Man is infinitely more complex than a galaxy. It's the Great Ordainer who introduces order into this world.

84

The assymmetry between the infinitely small and the infinitely large is indisputable. A sign of the presence of the infinitely conscious.

85

The three infinities - the infinitely small, the infinitely large and the infinitely conscious - define nature's system of reference.

86

The three infinities are a manifestation, on nature's plane or that of trans-nature, of the infinity of Three.

87

There's a similarity in nature between the three infinities, just as there's a similarity in nature between space and time. We could therefore say "the-three-infinities" as we say "space-time."

88

The similarity in nature between the three infinities constitutes the rational basis of the general principle of Relativity.

To the three infinities of nature correspond the three infinities of trans-nature: the infinitely present, the infinitely potential and the infinitely middle.

The included middle ensures the possibility of an energizing exchange between the three infinities of trans-nature.

The difference between the quantum particle and man: the quantum particle is confined to intermediary nature.

"Natura fecit saltum" is a quantum proposition. "Natura non fecit saltum" is a comic affirmation, for it is resolutely anti-cosmic.

An easy enigma to solve: is the Great Silence hiding within the quantum void or the quantum void within the Great Silence?

The most precise non-predetermined direction: the quantum aleatory. It's preposterous to confuse "aleatory" with "chance." The quantum aleatory is constructive, it has a direction - the self-organisation of natural systems. "Chance" is merely the name of a faceless God, invented by binary thought in order to be shot down.

Nature is in perpetual oscillation between constraint and chance, which is why it always chooses the Hidden Third.

Spontaneity introduces an element of indeterminacy into any evolutionary process. Heisenberg's relations of uncertainty indicate that spontaneity is, in fact, effective within nature.

97

God is no determinist. The proof is that Laplace had no need of the God hypothesis, which explains why determinism ended up in the warehouses of history.

98

The opposite of chance isn't necessity but the possible.

99

The Valley of Astonishment is a quantum valley: contradiction and indeterminacy watch over the voyager.

100

One can postulate the existence of a general principle of indeterminacy, acting within all processes of reality. Its scientific basis is the universal presence of the unknown.

101

Those who explore a single point find more wonders than in an entire universe. For the universe was born from a single point, which is why within each point of this world a universe lies concealed.

102

Why are there only three dimensions of space and one dimension of time? Is nature less inventive than physicists and mathematicians?

103

When there's no longer a way out within space and time, the only remaining solution is necessarily utopian and atemporal, which is why the basis of reality is non-space and non-time.

104

One space-time is abolished by another. All space-times are abolished by the universally included middle. What remains?

105

"Veiled reality" is a fertile notion: it encourages us to seek Absolute Evidence. But if we believe we can reveal veiled reality we fall into the trap of nothingness. How many levels of reality are concealed within "veiled reality"?

106

The presentation at the Temple is not a representation.

107

A magnificent union of contradictions: the "topos atopos" of the ancients. The place of non-place, the space of non-space, the time of non-time. An asymptotic journey, always beginning all over again.

108

A comprehension of the notion of time is crucial not only for philosophy but also for our everyday lives. When tradition calls time "the Only Ideally Subjective Phenomenon," it goes further than all modern philosophies.

109

Time is the cosmic measure of change systems. Whoever says "measure," also acknowledges "he who measures."

110

What is time for an observer capable of simultaneously embracing all events in the universe?

111

Time as the Only Ideally Subjective Phenomenon - the basis for a future theory of relativity encompassing different levels of reality.

112

Everything has to submit to the effects of time, from the microbe to God.

113

The universe appeared, it is said, through a contraction of God. Is man a contraction of the universe? It could explain why earth is probably the only inhabited body in the universe. "Contraction" does not imply "center." Man as a contraction of the universe does not lead to an anthropocentric view of the universe, but rather its opposite: an anti-Copernican vision.

114

Jacob Boehme tells us that time resides within eternity. History and non-time, therefore, feed one another.

115

Without the impossible, the possible is merely a sadistic game, invented to justify the irreversibility of time.

116

The fate of our physical universe has been played with dice, within an infinitesimal fraction of time. A sign that we have time to create our own destiny.

117

Why is the reversibility of time so well concealed within the universe of the infinitely small? So as not to disturb the course of the stars.

118

What a pathetic waste of effort to "demonstrate" time's arrow! Why this fear of non-time? Why present one's tiny fantasy as a new vision of the world?

119

The infinity of time is the infinity of death, which is why the irreversibility of time is the greatest metaphysical scandal.

120

The disturbance brought about by the macrophysical observer induces the irreversibility of time.

121

Let's imagine nature and the universe without an observer for an instant. In this case, would time be reversible or irreversible?

122

How can you compare seven days of non-space and non-time with seven days of space and time? The only link could be, of course, the meta-number Seven.

123

Distrust of numbers, which we can make say anything, mustn't conceal the symbolic importance of meta-numbers. As trees should never conceal the forest.

124

Nature is an ensemble of incarnate symbols, which is why words can never exhaust the richness of symbols. They can, all the more, disembody them.

125

Nature has a double language: mathematical language and symbolic language, which is why it's so difficult for us to understand what it's trying to tell us.

126

A popularization of Peirce's theorem: the Three and the Seven are the two meta-numbers giving rise to all proportions of reason.

127

Abstraction is part of reality.

128

Nature engenders its own history. To talk about the history of the universe is therefore an abuse of language. The physical universe, human logic and the history of humanity are three facets of nature.

129

Two universal laws of gravitation and anti-gravitation govern different levels of reality. The law of universal gravitation acts within nature, whilst the law of anti-gravitation works within anti-nature. You can thus see why nature and anti-nature are so easily confused.

130

Is the fall of Adam the first manifestation of universal gravitation?

131

How could a hollow being take possession of this world? Unless the world is its master, because it too is hollow.

132

Falling towards nothingness, rising towards Absolute Evidence - opposite poles of universal gravitation.

133

Poetic antigravitation is as universal as physical gravitation.

134

Falling in love - is there a better expression of anti-gravitation?

135

A direct manifestation of the law of generalized universal gravitation: it's always easier to descend than to rise. One falls inexorably onto the nearest cosmos. Man alone escapes the pull of universal gravitation: he can fall from the bottom to the top.

136

The greatest massacre in the history of the universe: the ever-growing numbers of dead here on earth.

137

A horrible arithmetical vision. If you add together the number of those who've lived before us to the number of those who are going to live after us you obtain a round number: infinity. (Assuming of course, there's no disintegration of the proton or other cosmic cataclysms). Upon which the entire universe feeds.

138

An obvious arithmetical observation: in infinite time, there'll be an infinite number of living who have lived on earth and an infinite number of dead who will die on earth. Subtracting these infinite numbers gives us a finite number: the numbers of the living at any given instant. The condition for life on earth is therefore at this price: an infinite number of dead.

139

Does the universe really need an infinite number of living-beings-death-flesh in order to engender life? Or is everything merely an accident of infinity?

140

The idea that the earth is the universe's consciousness factory shocks both our sensibility and our vanity. Why? Do we have to keep everything for ourselves?

141

The continuous cooling of the universe represents a slow exit from potential hell. Our material universe is a relic-universe, cold and virtually empty. The only recent addition is the appearance of man. We were born into a starry tomb. And thus the universe became new again.

142

From all evidence, it's not man who invented the universe but rather the universe that invented man. Within the bubbling hell of the primordial universe man appeared like a dream from quantum particles. A quantum dream that should not be told to adults.

143

Who observed the universe before the invention of man? Future man.

144

A poetic image: the primordial universe described though a wave function of extraordinary complexity. Man, therefore, would have appeared through a reduction of the wave packet, the whole universe playing the role of observation instrument. This vision could put an end to endless quarrels: chance and necessity, determinism -indeterminacy, Darwinism - non-Darwinism, the innate and the acquired.

145

A supremely narcissistic act on the part of the universe: inventing man in order to see itself in another's gaze.

146

Man is a cosmic nuance. More than a chasm: a nuance.

147

Cosmic self-organization is the ultimate form of divine courtesy upholding, despite everything, the freedom of man.

148

Man hasn't been created, but rather invented. Through pure selfishness: to ensure the self-reproduction of the universe. This is how man became mortal.

149

From the time of the origin of time and space, non-differentiated energy consented to create a primordial couple: a particle and an anti-particle. To get out of hell's garden, this couple tasted the forbidden fruit reserved for non-differentiated energy. Original sin is therefore a quantum sin. From God against Lucifer.

150

A galaxy for a few people: a subtle cosmic economy.

151

Without voluntary suffering there's no consciousness. Is it for that, from reduction to reduction, that the universe led to man, in order that he take possession of the earth?

152

The ancients were right. The earth is the center of the universe, for it's the only known cosmic body where nature and anti-nature collide.

153

The asymmetry of cosmic matter - anti-matter has enabled us to have a home here on earth. Where will cosmic nature - anti-nature symmetry lead us?

154

The irreducible novelty of our cosmos: the interaction between man and nature.

155

Man has the privilege of being an incarnation of the triple structure of nature: supernature, intermediary nature and creaturely nature. Here re-sides all difference between man and a star: a star is merely one aspect of creaturely nature.

156

Creaturely man is a child of the stars. Self-born man reverses roles: it's the universe that is born from man.

157

If the appearance of man on earth is an accident, I'm left to deduce that the entire universe is an accident. To talk of the evolution of the universe is therefore an imposture. Pure and simple quantum cosmologists would have to claim the status of newspaper journalists.

158

Is man merely a synthetic image of the Great Ordainer?

159

The so fecund antagonistic contradiction between entropy and anthropy. Why does the possibility of invisible action creating order in the world make us so afraid?

160

To be added to the list of crimes against humanity: denying the cosmic origins of man.

161

The double nature of man: nature and anti-nature. The first nature of man corresponds to the natural movement of nature, that uses man for its own purposes. The second nature of man corresponds to the contrary movement of nature, that permits the evolution of man. The greatness of man consists of the recognition and acceptance of his double nature.

162

Man is the privileged participant at the cosmic theatre: he is at the same time actor, director and spectator.

163

To secrete the mental, project it outside ourselves, transform it into something entirely apart in order to take possession of the earth. Is this our cosmic role?

164

The role of man as good actor: the recognition, on his own scale, of the effect of laws common to all scales. Thus the play continues being performed.

The energizing information of the quantum void is uni-cosmic, whereas that of man is multi-cosmic. It's what saves man from the grip of nothingness.

Humanity can initiate the big bang for another universe. Unless, worn out by its dreams, it remains in deep sleep.

The self-destruction of the human species, which is always a possibility these days, would bring about the destruction of the entire cosmos.

The supreme mechanical act: the suicide of a computer.

Our hatred of nature finds expression in the destruction of scale. Our lives are no longer set by the two great cosmic scales: the relationship between the age of humanity and the age of the universe, and the relationship between the lifetime of man and the age of humanity. Thus, prisoners of space and time, we believe we're their masters.

Why are there so many suns, yet so few beings of light?

The universe has taken billions of years to invent man and the earth. Whereas man in less than a century has given himself the means to destroy the earth entirely. An eloquent demonstration of man's impotence.

A simple definition of life: rediscovering our cosmic origins, finding our cosmic place, taking action.

173

There is no cosmic code - a fantasy invented to reassure us of our destination.

174

The angel is, of course, neither man nor beast. Between the two without becoming anything, eliminated by a game of possibles within a contraction of the universe. Have angels been eliminated by natural selection?

175

It's in the interest of perfection not to be of this world.

176

Nature allows man to feel intellectual rejoicing in complexity in order to then taste the living joy of simplicity. There is no other path to understanding.

177

What's the relationship between the imagination of man and the imagination of nature? It's certainly not a question of identity. So what is it?

178

Nature invents, man discovers. But when man invents, nature invents itself.

179

The ternary of attention is isomorphic to the ternary of nature. The attention of creatural nature watches over the action of homogenization. The attention of intermediary nature makes possible the action of heterogenization. As to the attention of supernature, it's nothing more than the universally present gaze of the Hidden Third.

180

The hypnotic power of reality: the killing of attention.

181

Nature is the living matrix of all phenomena, all philosophies, all religions, which is why a religion that neglects nature denies itself.

182

Nature is, by nature, transdisciplinary.

183

The major difficulty of concordism: one single nature, several religions.

184

The unnatural marriage of Christian thought with Aristotelian thought is a simple error of logic.

185

There are three kinds of sciences corresponding with three aspects of nature: exact sciences that study creatural nature, social sciences (including mathematics and theology) that study intermediary nature and sciences of the Hidden Third (including the philosophy of nature) that study supernature.

186

The opposition between nature and culture is absurd. For nature, the womb of all wombs, engenders culture. Without nature, culture is merely a forlorn word that deserves to die.

187

Nature and philosophy - who is servant and who is master? The master is definitely elsewhere.

188

Intermediary nature is the kingdom of the philosophy of nature. The philosophy of nature is a hard science, whereas other philosophies, in the majority of cases, are soft sciences. Hard nature confronting a soft brain.

189

The basis for a new philosophy of nature: nature as trans-nature.

190

The researcher - be it a scientific researcher, researcher of truth or re-searcher of God - can only be a heretic. Quite simply because nature is itself a heretic.

191

Nature is a kind of aesthete of cosmic sexuality. With the difference that it perpetually lives out its fantasies. The philosophy of nature could therefore be the poetics of cosmic sexuality.

192

A crowd of theoreticians of cosmic sexuality transform acts into words. A very tiny number of experimenters of cosmic sexuality transform words into acts. The disproportion of their number is a necessity: one cannot exist without the other.

193

The cosmic role of man is to keep watch, in order that the light of Abso-lute Evidence never goes out.

1

The only thing that's really worth seeking in this world is the Hidden Third.

2

Ambiguity rules the world. What greater ambiguity than that of "yes" and "no"?

3

The so current confusion between the included middle and ambiguity is engendered by the infinite ambiguity of binary thought.

4

Binary thought is one of several possible pathways towards truth. The false appearance of truth is a useful passion. The imposture of binary thought: not knowing its place. I don't wish to demonize binary thought, it's already demonic enough though extremely useful. I want, quite simply, to restore it to its rightful place.

5

Does the duality of life and death lie at the origin of binary thought?

6

By its own nature, the mental can't comprehend the language of the Hidden Third, which is why it proclaims its non-existence.

7

The logic of the excluded middle is adapted to describe a single level of reality. It's therefore necessary and useful: it makes us survive. But it also prevents us from living.

8

The sorrowfully included middle means "being seated between two chairs." A chasm of nothingness. Someone, who without being stupid, has never experienced the Hidden Third is not intelligent. He's seated between two chairs.

9

Non-sense is a sign of the absence of the Hidden Third. It can make us go round *ad vitam aeternam.*

10

Binary logic is deadly. Always seek the Hidden Third.

11

The suicide of an individual, the suicide of a nation or the suicide of humanity are merely the outcome (and triumph) of binary logic.

12

Wealth is a spectacular visualization of the Hidden Third's exclusion. Wars, revolutions, famine, hatred are mere complements of this image. The hidden source is always binary logic.

13

Occultism and technoscience share one common characteristic: an attempt to kill the Hidden Third. Power for the sake of power.

14

Triviality conceals its binary game very well, for it presents itself as a crossroads where only three pathways lead.

15

A renowned pianist often asks his students: What lies between two notes in a score? Invariably the students respond: nothing. Their professor tells them they're mistaken: between the two notes lies the first note. But he too is mistaken: between two notes there's nothing, plus the first note.

16

The evil words of binary thought - curse words - an opening towards the chasm of non-sense.

17

Within the infinite void of the excluded middle the stupidity of the world is swallowed up.

18

The wonderful but painful journey from the so sorrowfully excluded middle towards the land of the Hidden Third.

19

To conceive the world as a waiting room: a room of the lost footsteps of the Hidden Third.

20

What is empty is full, what is full is empty, between the two falls our gaze.

21

Living by middles, dying by middles - what's the difference? The Hidden Third is not an intermediary of middles.

22

Echoes at all levels of reality - the birth of the Hidden Third.

23

Is it a coincidence if "fléau" means at the same time "part upon which rests the pans of the weighing scales" as well as "cataclysm, catastrophe, disaster"? The blinding of the included middle is a cosmic malfunctioning.

24

The Hidden Third may be nothing more than a perpetual movement between evolution and involution.

25

Different facets of the Hidden Third: time and non-time, autonomy and constraint, separable and non-separable, visible and invisible, manifested and non-manifested, continuity and discontinuity, local causality and global causality, the wave and the corpuscle, symmetry and the breaking of symmetry, the reversibility and irreversibility of time.

26

In our information era everything is confused. The Great Ordainer ("Grand Ordinateur") is not a computer. Only man has the privilege of living the secret code of the included middle.

27

The Hidden Third is like light. Its motion is the same in all reference systems.

28

The most accessible sign of the included middle: the impossibility of manipulation.

29

Man and the universe are participants in meaning as ternary.

30

Unity in diversity and diversity through unity cannot exist without the discontinuity of the included middle.

31

There are three kinds of knowledge: scientific knowledge, experiential knowledge and knowledge of the Hidden Third. The meeting between these three forms gives rise to different levels of knowledge.

32

Ternary contradiction is, in its unity, a-spatial, a-temporal and a-logical. But its self-interaction engenders space, time and logic.

33

The holy ternary: that which is without-place, that which is without-time and endlessness.

34

The most difficult ternary to grasp lies beyond words: being, non-being and endlessness.

35

"Seeing" suggests the light of reason's ternary: physical light, the light of the soul as well as the dark light of endlessness. One without the other is blind.

36

The double nature of nature, the double nature of attention, the double nature of man - the basis for a trialectical structure of the world.

37

The word trialectic has been coined to distinguish the false ternary of the sorrowfully excluded middle from the authentic ternary of the Hidden Third, which could be why it triggers so much passion.

38

Why did Raymond Abellio react with so much vehemence against the trialectic? Perhaps the author of The Absolute Structure perceived with great lucidity the infinitely intoxicating dizziness engendered by the Hidden Third.

39

Science is certainly no substitute for a spiritual path, but it's the royal road towards the narrow way of the Hidden Third.

40

One facet of intelligence: making a choice ("legere") that lies between ("inter") two possible choices. Intelligence and the included middle are therefore indissociable.

41

The secret weapon of the included middle: the poetic word.

42

The language of the Hidden Third is a foreign language: it ought to be taught in school.

43

Someone who talks the language of the Hidden Third isn't a clown ("fumiste") but rather sensational ("fumant"): a sign of the great fire of Absolute Evidence.

44

The only universal language is the one of the Hidden Third. No-one will ever succeed in inventing it.

45

The language of Jesus is the one of the Hidden Third, which is why he was crucified.

46

Jesus was somewhat surrounded by women for they understand better than men the language of the Hidden Third.

47

Why are the persons of the Trinity never represented by women?

48

The secret link between the Virgin and the included middle: the Sophia.

49

The genius of Christianity - giving a body to the included middle.

50

Binary thought has created an opposition between believers and un-believers. The thinking of the Hidden Third replaces this opposition with the contradictory interaction between intelligence and negligence.

51

The divine ternary - death to oneself, mirror of nature, birth of God - is at the same time the source and result of all other ternaries.

52

The bootstrap of ternaries: every ternary is what it is because all other ternaries exist at the same time. A heretical conclusion: the divine ternary has no privileged place.

53

The energy - movement - relation triad rules the world.

54

There is indeed a misunderstanding of evil: evil understands ternary vibrations.

55

The Hidden Third, generally, has nothing to do with ternaries or triads. Often the ternary is merely a sophisticated form of the binary. You can go back as far as the Great Triad yet find no trace of the Hidden Third.

56

Another false ternary: father, mother, child. The anti-model of the Hidden Third.

57

Beware of the Great Imitator - he often takes on a ternary form to make us believe in the presence of the Hidden Third. Thesis, antithesis, synthesis - the Great Triad of the Great Imitator.

58

The ternary is merely one possible manifestation of the Hidden Third. An example of a binary where the included middle is present: transdisciplinarity /anti -transdisciplinarity.

59

All disputes regarding the precedence of the ternary or quaternary seem to me to be in vain: the ternary gives rise to the quaternary, whereas the quaternary decomposes into triads, which is why the cross has the appearance of a quaternary.

60

The basis of binary logic: the distinction between man and woman. The original sin.

61

Trisexuality is the basis for human rights.

62

All human beings are trisexual. Neither, man, woman nor androgyne - trisexual.

63

Those who proclaim themselves bisexual do it out of a taste for aesthetic provocation. Perfect proof that they are in fact trisexual.

64

Love is not a representation but the presence of the Hidden Third.

65

The sexual act understood as a celebration of the Hidden Third. So-called "sexual liberation" - what a great illusion...

66

They talk of a single ("Un") male metaphysic. But a single ("Une") female metaphysic is also necessary for the generation of the many. In the light of the Hidden Third.

67

A major default in so many domains of knowledge, including quantum mechanics: they have several founding fathers but no founding mother.

68

Trisexuality is trialectic. The sexological is not, therefore, an insult to love.

69

Without woman, man is nothing. A woman can say as much as a man. An implicit acknowledgement of the third sex.

70

The sexuality of the Hidden Third is not yet developed within being, which is why we only see men and women around us. The paradox of the third sex: the receptacle is perfectly developed, but can still remain empty.

71

Beings of the third sex impregnate men as well as women. And they in turn must be impregnated. Otherwise we'd call them masters.

72

Transmission is a trans-mission.

73

The teacher ("Le Maître") is the one who masters his own ignorance, which is why he can be impregnated by the Hidden Third.

74

An open mind feeds on all knowledge past, present and future, which is why true teachers are so rare. So-called "disciples" of an open mind only swallow up the thought of the teacher, deform and caricature it and thus end up feeding off a corpse.

75

A true teacher can not have disciples, only companions. He stimulates his companions to become, in their turn, teachers.

76

The teacher always needs servants in order to accomplish his task. But humiliated, the servants rebel and kill the teacher. This tragic paradox has only one solution - completely utopian and therefore realistic: we become masters and servants of one another. When we all become masters, the earth will rediscover its being. A definitive abolition of war will be the outcome.

The relationship between wisdom and trisexuality is so obvious we don't see it.

The mystical is the expression of a feminine polarity. Gnosis - one of a masculine polarity. Which is the path of the Hidden Third? Certainly not science, which is an androgynous path.

What are monks for? For preserving the amorous relationship between Monos and Una. Guardians of trisexuality.

We're all brothers before the Hidden Third, which is why the world is a great invisible monastery.

The Hidden Third is the third term of Absolute Evidence.

1

Deifying nature, naturalizing God, affirming non-duality, proving the existence of God, denying God, postulating that nature = God, taking nature or God as a source for all possible responses - multiple manifestations of one and the same logic: binary logic.

2

From the dawn of time everything has been written and said about divinity and divinities, God and gods, their presence and absence, their existence and non-existence. Why is nature always forcing us to start all over again?

3

Why choose between "Elohim" and "God": a simple question about the nationality of words. The singular lies within the plural: the plural within the singular.

4

The word "God" doesn't bother me, given that it's not a hypothesis.

5

What a tragi-comic spectacle: all these nihilists, atheists and scientists as well as all these fanatical believers who crowd like beggars at the doors of the sacred! Without feeding on God's corpse they couldn't survive.

6

Why are all the atheists I know, with only one exception, really anti-theists? As for the one who is a true atheist, I can't name him.

7

A trick of man to rid himself of God: inventing human mathematics. Thus he falls into his own trap.

8

Some say God is the ego made absolute, but it's precisely the ego that says that.

9

The humility of monks who refuse to talk about God is suspect. A supreme ruse of binary thought: identifying ignorance with transcendence.

10

If only my great friend knew how much I understand him when he tells me he wants to reach for his gun every time he hears the word "God"! Nature is beyond words, my dear friend, but at least we can say the word "nature."

11

"God" is a proper noun, "transcendence" a substantive and "cosmic" an adjective. Anything else is mere chatter.

12

There are three kinds of religions: religions of terrestrial salvation that put man in the place of God in order to kill him; religions of divine salvation that put God in the place of man in order to kill him; and religions based upon the principle of relativity, which quite simply puts man in his place.

13

Basically, religions of all ages have tried to find the key to one and the same enigma: how such an exalted light could find refuge within such rottenness? But there is no key because there's no enigma.

14

The greatest worshippers of God are those that deny him.

15

Proving God(s) through science is an imposture, for that's a confusion of places. Proving science through God(s), therefore, is also an imposture. The only position, in accordance with laws, is research of science by science.

16

The pathways of logic are impenetrable: saying the world is a hoax of the gods is sacrilege, however, saying gods are a hoax of the world is acceptable.

17

This world is a strange performance: birth is free, the price of admission is death, the director's a group of actors, the text hasn't been written, the spectators are invisible. As to the play's author, he's merely a topic of conversation.

18

Why choose between God and Gods? God has at least three faces and all gods are linked by the same logic. Monotheism and polytheism - another fantasy engendered by binary thought. Of course there is, as always, a third possibility.

19

Theology is the science of God's orgasm.

20

When I write "God" I mean the plural. When I write "gods" I mean the singular. When I write nothing I mean nothingness.

21

Infinite exhilaration, infinite giddiness, infinite lucidity: three keywords for approaching God's orgasm.

22

The quantum void is a meeting between being and non-being. The visible world is being within non-being: the invisible world is non-being within being, which is why nothing can exhaust the riches of the quantum void. For it is nothingness.

23

From orgasm to orgasm God is born.

24

Knowledge ("connaissance") is a joint birth ("co-naissance"). The birth of God and the birth of man.

25

Divine tragedy: God's sacrifice permits the birth of man. But at a price: the birth of God.

26

An accumulation of cosmological data can say nothing about God's orgasm. Except that it's a plausible event.

27

Those who want to make God work remain where they are. Those who are worked by God advance. This is the origin of movement.

28

God is a god of order, said Jakob Boehme. A god who plays with dice, a god who manipulates disorder to create order. The god who plays with dice is the god of Socratic dialogue.

29

The Great Separator gives us the illusion of a universe of pure order or pure disorder. This devil with two faces is merely one facet of God.

30

The Devil is the greatest ally of God in the Great Game of Socratic dialogue. "Diabolos" means "one who divides," which is why the Great Separator is so useful to the unity of the world.

31

The Devil is a cosmic necessity: an immense energizing power station of disorder from which order can be engendered.

32

The conversion of the Devil would be a cosmic catastrophe.

33

The Great Indeterminate - the God who plays with dice. "The old don't play dice" - wrote Einstein in a letter to Bohr. Einstein was wrong: and old, and game.

34

The unity of the undefined sequence of cosmoses escapes the effect of time, it is. Which is why God is subject to the effects of time.

35

Archeologists of the universe attempt to piece together God's orgasm starting from relics. Like the blind describing a white elephant through touching different parts of its body.

36

The numeric value of the relationship between the lifetime of man and the lifetime of the universe is proof that man has been created in the image of God.

37

Distinguishing God's orgasm from the cosmic orgasm. The pressure of the cosmic orgasm - the appearance of our universe, is followed by cosmic depression - the appearance of man. God's orgasm represents eternal genesis of the plurality of cosmoses.

38

The universe's delusions of grandeur create galaxy upon galaxy, with no apparent use. Man's delusions of grandeur engender fantasy upon fantasy, which are just as uneconomical. Must we conclude that our planet is itself the product of fantasy?

A heretical question: what is the role of the Sophia in God's orgasm?

Why are God-the-father, the Holy Spirit, Jesus, the Virgin Mary, the saints or the angels never shown laughing? The absence of laughter - a sign of divine depression? Happily there are some smiles.

Cosmic laughter - the cosmic orgasm.

It was Lupasco who introduced the expression "God's orgasm." One of the most wonderful Lupascian dreams: a universe of the T state (the T of the included middle - "tiers inclus"). Beings, planets, suns, galaxies, stars in the T state. A permanent cosmic orgasm.

A bizarre ternary: God, the Devil, Man. Its cosmic role is an energising loop: from ignorance of nothingness to knowledge of nothingness.

Between nothingness and everything - our own lives.

Scientific knowledge - a minute description of God's orgasm; experiential knowledge - allowing oneself to be penetrated by God. Poetic knowledge - a celebration of God's orgasm.

Forgetting that the word "God" is present within the word "enthusiasm" - a manifestation of negligence. A superb example of the prostitution of words.

Enthusiasm means being inspired or possessed by divinity. Why this suspicion of enthusiasm? Is penetration by God so painful?

48

Is there a higher communion than God's orgasm? God's orgasm is a poetic explosion - a big bang of the indescribable.

49

The omnipotence of God wouldn't know how to limit itself to just one orgasm.

50

The world is either the kingdom of death, or the kingdom of affectivity. When the orgasm of affectivity makes everything tremble, the world will be born.

51

What is God? asks a child looking at itself in a mirror. Its own gaze responds. What is nature? asks a physicist looking at his equations. The mathematical symbols respond. What is man? asks man, contemplating his immense power on this planet. Here, there's no response.

52

There's no proof of God, because God is Absolute Evidence.

1

It's not God who creates problems, but man.

2

The birth of our universe has as its goal the self-birth of man, which explains why the earth is so ridiculously small and full whilst our galaxy is so large and empty.

3

The new birth represents a transition from one level of materiality towards another. Why does this new birth deviate so far from terrestrial birth?

4

The strategy of the universe is the birth of man. The strategy of man is his new birth. A work greater than that of the universe.

5

We're all under high surveillance from the stars. How do we escape this cosmic prison?

6

The self-consistency of the universe requires the conjoined self-birth of man and God.

7

Incarnation remains a great mystery: disembodiment is certain, whereas reincarnation remains very hypothetical.

8

Terrestrial birth is the anti-model of the new birth, which is why it's so indispensible.

9

Perfect symmetry: the work of God - the self-birth of God, the work of man - the self-birth of man. It is, in fact, the same work.

10

The only horrible suffering: the separation of God from himself. The founding act of our joie de vivre. The ultimate generosity: the sacrifice of self-genesis.

11

Why does the immanence of death conceal the eminence of life to such an extent?

12

We live through questions. We die through answers, which is why we have unanswerable questions.

13

Become a question yourself.

14

The source of life is life and the source of death is death, which is why life begins where life ends.

15

Ahead of us: death, behind us: life - what lies in-between?

16

Is man a complicated accident, an accidental complexity or an accident of complexity? Absurd Evidence is the question linking all these questions. Without words, without thought and with no response.

17

Entropic death, anthropic life - where is the Hidden Third?

18

We live quietly with the danger of death every day of our lives, which is why we've no time for the danger of life.

19

The danger of life is a putting to death of everyday death. All riches giving meaning to everyday death are threatened, which is why we experience life as danger.

20

We didn't ask for life, yet we refuse death. We didn't ask for death yet we refuse life.

21

At the corpse's banquet only death clinks glasses. At the banquet of the living, death serves up the elixir of life.

22

The only interesting aspect of life on earth is death. The passion of the dead is for corpses. The passion of the living is for death. The passion of death is life.

23

"Danger: life!" should be displayed in all public places throughout the world.

24

The role of our everyday orgasms ("la petite mort") is to make us live for the great death ("la grande mort").

25

Death is the sleep of reason, whereas life is its awakening, which is why, if we really want to live, we have to think every day of our own death.

26

Man has been spared immortality in order that he can live. Thus knowledge has been given to him.

27

Immortality signifies the unchanging, which is why entropy and death were invented by nature.

28

Death is the absence of energy-giving exchange, which is why it's not inevitable.

29

The immediate actuality of life demonstrates all the vanity of the journalists of being.

30

Our so-called "life" is merely a long sleep. We can thus understand why the danger of life is felt, more or less unconsciously, as being considerably greater than the danger of death.

31

The importance of our lives lies in making the impossible possible. Life takes care of everything else.

32

Non-life is not death, which is why a quantum particle contains within it all the life of the universe.

33

Entropic fascination finds its outcome in death. Without opening there is no salvation. The increase of entropy is merciless.

34

An arithmetical question: if an infinitesimal fraction of a second sufficed to build, potentially, an entire physical universe, how many universes could we engender within the life of a man?

35

There's much talk of a demographic crisis amongst the living, but they forget the one of the dead. There are so many dead here on earth that soon there'll no longer be any room for the living.

36

There's only one metaphysical problem, with two faces: death and sleep.

37

The ontological basis of sleep: the confusion between the afterlife and the over-life ("la survie et la sur-vie").

38

Our sleep is like a quantum void: it contains within it, potentially, an entire universe.

39

Is sleep more comfortable than waking? Do earth and the whole universe have a vested interest in plunging us into endless sleep?

40

The shortest path between life and death is sleep.

41

The sleep of man is forgetfulness of his poetic origin. A sleep worse than death.

42

The true meaning of suicide: negligence of attention.

43

What are the cosmic roots of sleep and those of awakening? Is sleep the cardinal sin of man, or of awakening?

44

A wise man tells us to awaken, to die, to be born. A concise description of the new birth. Does an entire lifetime suffice to wander this long path?

45

Death to oneself is neither a right, nor an obligation of man. It's the price to pay for avoiding death.

46

The meaning of life: the world reduced to one and the same question.

47

The capacity to listen - the greatest achievement of the human psyche.

48

To consider the history of humanity as the history of a long sleep. But whoever says "sleep" also says "waking" and even "awakening." Therefore the history of humanity could be a prehistory to awakening.

49

War - a conflict between the living dead.

50

Responsibility is a question of love, which is why we can give birth to ourselves. The impotence of robots: self-genesis is impossible for them. Robots give birth, at most, to other robots. Robotics is the science of the non-engendering of self.

51

If reproduction of the species is our goal, then we become the annex of our sex. If new birth is our aspiration, then sex is the most precious of our servants. Love of the excluded middle: sex as master. Love of the Hidden Third: sex as servant.

52

Conversion is a simple energising process: the transformation of nature into anti-nature.

53

Our daily bread serves our daily death. The bread which the "Our Father" speaks of, therefore, is of another degree of materiality.

54

The coming of man is, above all, experience.

55

Irreversible time is the immortality of death. Which time serves the immortality of life?

56

The ancients certainly understood that we're all consumed by time. That is to say by our own creation. But such evidence puts into question the comfort of our everyday death, which is why we invented such a powerful self-tranquilizer: objective time.

57

Some say time is made for imbeciles. Non-time too.

58

Man can not only produce time but also turn back or even abolish time, which is why he's not only a producer of non-sense but also anti-sense and even sense.

59

Only the new birth escapes the irreversibility of time, like the creation and annihilation of quantum particles.

60

I'm fascinated by wingless angels: to me they seem to symbolize the idea that angels are already made, with no becoming.

61

We are all the same age as our souls. There are newborns and those who are not yet born. All my best friends are children.

62

Great artists, great philosophers, great scholars, great prophets of all eras, were they all newborns?

63

Life is a perpetual fluctuation between Absurd Evidence and Absolute Evidence. The two pillars of wisdom.

64

The ternary of life: the life of everyday death, the life of the new birth and the life of the Hidden Third. The unity of this ternary is the life of life.

65

The question of life is simple: being born.

66

There is no life after death. There is life after life and death after death.

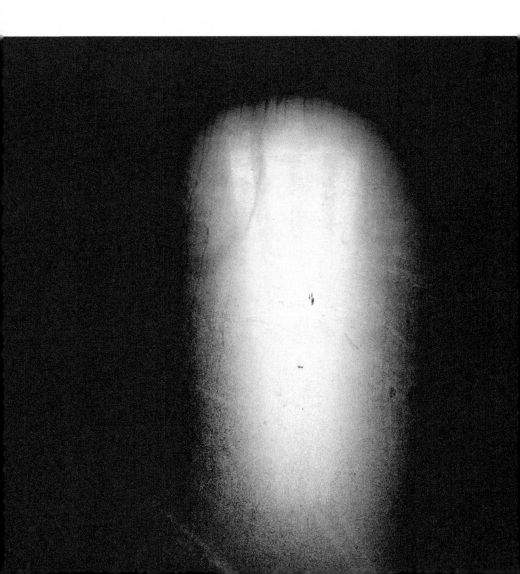

1

If it's true the problem of meaning has no meaning, I pray all actors be willing to leave the stage. The stage labelled "I."

2

What if we reverse roles, and it's for God to prove the existence of man. Relieved of a serious problem, we could thus begin our quest.

3

Inner being can only appear through an immense a-spatial, a-temporal, a-logical void, that feeds upon space, time and logic.

4

The shortest path from the infinitely small to the infinitely large is through the infinitely conscious.

5

There's only one true initiation: self-initiation. Its goal: the meeting with oneself, having undergone the ordeals of the infinitely small and the infinitely large.

6

If you can answer the question "what is your passion?," you've already started on the journey.

7

Occurrences of being arise within inner silence like virtual particles in the quantum void. Thus cosmoses are born.

8

The only holy war worthy of the name is the journey. The journey from one level of reality towards another.

9

To finally accept the obvious: I am not. Otherwise, why embark on the long voyage in search of the Simorgh?

The distance from oneself to oneself is greater than the radius of the universe, which is why it can't be abolished by space or time.

Beyond the singular and plural: trans-presence.

Responsibility consists of taking control of conjugating the verb "to be."

If I am - you are, he/she is, we are, you (plural) are, they are, the universe is. The conjugation of verbs is always asymmetrical.

The greatest responsibility of all: the transmission of mystery.

" 'To be' is to be connected," said Alfred Korzybski. Without the opening towards the unknown there's no freedom.

The complicity of looking: 1) I look at a tree; 2) All of a sudden I feel the presence of something watching me whilst looking at the tree; 3) The tree, in turn, starts looking at me. Thus the ternary nature of looking is accomplished.

Knowledge begins with the exploration of attention. The look behind the look - attention's double nature.

The Great Silence is in fact limitless attention: a contemplation of all cosmoses past, present and future within the mirror of wisdom.

19

Attention is a negentropic phenomenon. The more preoccupied we become with attention, the more entropy decreases. The more attention we give to worldly things, the more entropy increases. Negentropy is engendered by the presence of attention. To wait ("attendre") means "to be attentive." The unexpected ("inattendu") is therefore attention's higher presence.

20

A stroke of luck: attention and a-tension are indissociable. Jean-Pierre Brisset rightly said: "Satan" really means "it tends" ("Satan"/"ça tend").

21

The Devil tells me: Go to the Devil! God tells me: Go to the Devil! Who to believe?

22

One possible meaning of freedom: not giving attention to anything, but rather allowing oneself to be possessed & carried away by attention. Or to put it another way, you can't give what you haven't got.

23

The great unknown: ourselves. Or at least a really true image. When the mirror's not broken.

24

Being is subject to the general principle of indeterminacy. The advent of being is indeterminate, instantaneous, unpredictable, even if it requires a concurrence of very precise conditions.

25

Everything that surrounds us - the invisible rendered visible. Our task: to go in the opposing direction.

26

The discovery of the unknown is a sudden meeting with oneself. The opposite of narcissism.

27

Within the heart of being are the letters of nature.

28

The known is the way towards the unconscious, whereas the unknown is the way towards consciousness.

29

A simple definition of consciousness: the only non-degradable energy, passing from nowhere to nowhere.

30

The only interesting thing we can expect is the unexpected. The unexpected has a quantum nature, which is why its waiting rooms are almost empty.

31

The inner teacher is the messenger of being. Other teachers are messengers of the messenger.

32

Is there any teacher apart from the inner teacher? More precisely, teachers are those who have witnessed the birth of their own inner teacher.

33

A teaching without a teacher is like a virgin without a hymen. A teacher without a teaching - the same.

34

Inner riches are like external riches. You can only give to the rich. A happy consolation: the universe belongs to the poorest.

35

A particle accelerator is, of course, visible whereas a consciousness accelerator is invisible. But their goal is the same: very high energies.

36

It's logical that vows uttered at religion's door form a ternary: poverty, obedience, chastity - for this ternary is isomorphic to the divine ternary.

37

The vow of poverty is very simple to carry out: relinquish all riches brought about by an exclusion of the Hidden Third.

38

The vow of obedience means lending a sympathetic ear to oneself. The only difficulty: having a good ear.

39

The vow of chastity means participating in God's orgasm.

40

Non-identification is the other name for vision.

41

The meaning of terrestrial prison: not allowing oneself, at any price, to be confined by the simplicity of an answer or the complexity of a question. Thus, one can understand why the simplest questions give rise to answers of an infinite complexity.

42

The great cosmic unification ought to begin with a very tiny unification, that of man himself. How can a non-unified physicist conceive a Great Unification Theory?

43

An action carried out in knowledge conjoins with inaction.

44

The price of reason is madness: the price of madness awakening.

45

Zeami really is a quantum thinker: he attracts our attention to the importance of intervals of non-interpretation separating two gestures, two actions, two movements. It's within this quantum leap of non-interpretation that we can really play our role as actors of life.

46

Masks are keepers of the world's equilibrium.

47

Knocking down masks is a salutary act, providing there's something behind the masks.

48

Our true face is cosmic, which is why any mask is comic, tragic, tragicomic or even without movement.

49

A bad actor is like a puppet in the hands of his own masks. For a good actor masks are merely a necessary means for making our own face appear.

50

The forgetting of oneself by oneself gives rise to monsters.

51

A centerpiece in the museum of cosmic caricatures: "Me, I am."

52

The tyranny of the mental makes us blind to the Hidden Third.

53

Anyone who's never experienced the drunkenness of ideas has understood nothing of this world. As for the one who can't get beyond the drunkenness of ideas, the world is not worthy of him.

54

A good definition of hell: forever going round in circles.

55

Indeed, all coffins are empty. Or filled with masks that are no longer of any use. Except for maintaining appearances.

56

Perhaps our space-time is merely a sub-division of a far richer space-time. Are we all life prisoners in the prison of our own space-time?

57

Everything arrives too early or too late: life, love, death. There's only one thing that always arrives on time: non-time.

58

Quadridimensional reality is endless, because it's always giving rise to itself. The prisoner's only hope: making the utopian, atemporal seeds anchored deeply within him come to fruition.

59

The tautological is the most effective self-tranquilizer. It alone can give a name to the meaning of life.

60

There's a gulf between being present and making present. The gulf between presentation and representation.

61

Where does this unhealthy confusion between provocation and Socratic dialogue come from? A visceral fear of the included middle?

62

The puppets' good fortune - allowing themselves to be guided, with no effort. Puppets never tire.

63

Those who fear infinity have never explored the endlessness of the finite.

64

Puppets can never pull strings. But they do have the privilege of believing they can.

65

Suicide is a false problem. Whatever Albert Camus says, it's not a philosophical but rather a logical problem. Answering "yes" or "no" to the question "consider whether your life is or isn't worth living" amounts to placing yourself within a very specific kind of logic - binary logic.

66

Suicide as tautology: why commit suicide when you're already dead?

67

The problem with problems is that there'll always be problems. Whilst allowing problems to resolve themselves we can take the time to live.

68

What is "living" if not allowing discontinuity to act within oneself.

69

We've been told, from the dawn of time, that what's up above resembles what's down below. But no-one tells us what's in-between.

70

Even if I knew the complete organization chart for heaven, nobody could show me the way towards myself. Above all not God.

71

The one who seeks finds. And the one who finds finds nothing, which is why the seeker's destiny is always to seek.

72

How do we help God? Why within the secrecy of our inner life do we discern without any ambiguity this imperious demand for help?

73

A stranger from birth, my world is nature.

74

I feel no need to believe: fidelity towards nature suffices me. I dream of a world in search of its nature.

75

What's the difference between conquest and quest? The outcome of a quest is the opposite of conquest.

76

Don't shoot mutants. They're only following quantum law.

77

The non-reproducible rediscovery of the occurrences of being - a wonder of reason.

78

We're all voyagers of the unknown, in search of our forgotten king, the Simorgh.

The greatest painting of all: one that allows us to see the ultimate color of our being.

Create silence within yourself so that all the potentiality of the real can come to fruition - strange quantum alchemy.

All the voyager risks whilst heading into the unknown is the loss of his own chains.

Our true face is the asymptotic limit of an infinite series of masks. It's therefore pure potentiality. Its emergence within reality corresponds with an energizing miracle - that of cosmic unity.

A child asks me: what did my face resemble before I was born? Without hesitation I reply: what did my face resemble before I was born?

Inner silence is like the quantum void. Everything becomes possible. Even the universe, even life.

Man's supreme gift: trans-substantiation.

Everything begins with passion. Beyond passion there's love, beyond love: friendship, beyond friendship: self-knowledge, beyond self-knowledge: nothing, beyond nothing: everything, beyond everything: the mirror of our own face. The highest love: contemplation of one's own face. The opposite of narcissism, which is merely the contemplation of a mask. The perfect mask is one of stillness. It permits a life without masks to arise.

87

Why does such an innocent game of mirrors - seeing yourself as you are - strike such fear? Why is the path from oneself to oneself virtually inaccessible?

88

The Simorgh is our own face illuminated by the triple light of nature within the mirror of the Great Indeterminate.

89

My true friends bring me life: the Hidden Third appears within the mirror of the Other.

90

The definition of sincerity is simple: seeing yourself, opening your heart to the other, acknowledging and living according to cosmic laws. One should start learning sincerity at nursery school. Thus the world would become more bearable.

91

Knowing yourself - what a strange paradox. How can you know yourself without being known?

92

Some are surprised that the infinitely small and the infinitely large are so well described by mathematics, while the macrophysical scale evades such description. This is precisely where the chasm of the infinitely conscious is found.

93

Inner silence is a kind of asceticism. Word fasts should be organised across the world on a regular basis. Give up words. Make them sacred.

94

My final wish. To be buried beneath all the books I never read.

95

I try finding myself everywhere where I'm not.

96

When you swim on the surface you're not in danger of life but you are in danger of power.

97

A to-do list of urgent things: the accomplishment of desires, accumulation of riches and knowledge, doing the same as everyone else, esteem, forgetting death, always going faster, loving, hating, ruling over others (the list is endless). And, if there's enough time, living.

98

I have an embarrassment of choices: a rag doll, a stone statue, dust. Not choosing, therefore, is an act of rudimentary dignity.

99

An arithmetical problem: a third of the body isn't the included middle ("le tiers inclus"), a third of feeling isn't the included middle, a third of the intellect isn't the included middle. It's the harmonization of all three that makes the Hidden Third arise.

100

What makes me live: whatever lies between images, between words, between thoughts. Within the emptiness of thought, within the emptiness of feeling, within the emptiness of the body arises the plenitude of life.

101

The emergence of being is the sudden discovery of simplicity within complexity.

102

The symbol only has meaning through its interactions with all other symbols, which is why it only dwells within the secrecy of inner life.

103

When I'm open, millions and millions of new ideas are constantly presenting themselves to me. Their brilliance accounts for their instant oblivion. Their brilliance, or their other-worldliness.

104

My only regret at not being immortal: not being able to say everything I have to say. The supreme arrogance: the assumption that I'm the only person in the world capable of saying what I have to say.

105

Non-action is the supreme act. At its heart lies the quantum void containing potentially the whole universe.

106

Why do so few actors wear their inner lives on their faces? Isn't a good actor quite simply the one who finds his place within the movement of cosmic energy?

107

The sign of a successful quest: arriving nowhere.

108

The game - being: I.

109

The greatest poetic mystery: seeing one's own face for the very first time. At the threshold of the chamber of the Simorgh. A festival of mourning, a festival of birth.

110

The suddenness of the occurrence of being provides irrefutable proof of universal interdependence.

111

Those on spaceship Earth who stop at the beginning of the journey, return to dust. Those who, in the course of the journey, become frightened by the difficulties of the journey and stop, return to dust. Only the horsemen of the unknown stand a chance.

112

Within the glance of a small child there's an entire universe. Because it's not thinking. It is.

113

To know - to be known - to recognize - being born.

114

Our true face isn't the mask of the face. Behind the mask of the face there's the mask of the head, behind the mask of the head there's the mask of feeling, behind the mask of feeling there's the mask of the body, behind the mask of the body there's the mask of the face. Only anti-light beings can see our real face.

115

The feminine of I: Joy. Both words convey the same meaning: the entirety of being.

116

Joy is the measure of Absolute Reality; the first sign of its manifestation. Joy can never be saturated, for it feeds on Absolute Evidence.

117

One day someone will again emerge from the ranks to tell us everything is wrong and we will know he speaks the truth. Is it necessary for all that to shoot him, following the barbarous logic of non-contradiction?

118

When "I" embraces every cosmos with its light, it can finally say "I am."

To all living beings on earth and, above all, to friends who by their presence contributed to the destiny of this book: Domingo Adame, Adonis, L. M. Arcade, Gustavo Avilés, René Berger, Peter Brook, Michel Camus, Mircea Ciobanu, Michel de Salzmann, Lima de Freitas, Mircia Dumitrescu, Anne Henry, Vintila Horia, Clara Janés, Roberto Juarroz, Jacques Lacarrière, Alain Kremski, Stéphane Lupasco, Michelle Moreau, Edgar Morin, John Morton, Michel Random, Francis Rollet, Alexandru Rossetti, Horia Stamatu, Karen-Claire Voss.

In chapter six of this book, Basarab Nicolescu states that "the rigour of the poetic mind is infinitely greater than that of the mathematical mind." Certainly, from my own reading, *The Hidden Third* emerges as an epic poem for today, and it's very much in this spirit that I've translated its enigmatic (and poetic) theorems.

Wherever possible, I've tried to remain true to the short, succinct phrasings of the original, except where the conventions of the target language demanded otherwise. Unfortunately, not all of the word plays that worked so well in French have made the transition. In Chapter XIII, Theorem 20, for example, the sonic similarity between satan and ça tend ('Satan' and 'it tends,' respectively) is lost in English. Wherever such instances have occured, I've placed the original French words in brackets after the corresponding English version.

Finally, I would like to take this opportunity to thank Basarab Nicolescu, Marta del Pozo, Lissi Sánchez & all at Quantum Prose. As *The Hidden Third* reminds us, our highest responsibility is the transmission of mystery; something this translator has sought to keep in mind throughout.

William Garvin
09/03/15

Your Words Matter

Your Words Matter

CPSIA information can be obtained at www.ICGtesting.com
Printed in the USA
BVOW06s0345280916

463516BV00005B/15/P

9 780997 301403